How to use Questioning in the Classroom:

The Complete Guide

By Mike Gershon

Series Introduction

The 'How to...' series developed out of Mike Gershon's desire to share great classroom practice with teachers around the world. He wanted to put together a collection of books which would help professionals no matter what age group or subject they were teaching.

Each volume focuses on a different element of classroom practice and each is overflowing with brilliant, practical strategies, techniques and activities – all of which are clearly explained and ready-to-use. In most cases, the ideas can be applied immediately, helping teachers not only to teach better but to save time as well.

All of the books have been designed to help teachers. Each one goes out of its way to make educators' lives easier and their lessons even more engaging, inspiring and successful then they already are.

In addition, the whole series is written from the perspective of a working teacher. It takes account of the realities of the classroom, blending theoretical insight with a relentlessly practical focus.

The 'How to...' series is great teaching made easy.

Author Introduction

Mike Gershon has been creating resources for teachers since 2009. His twenty guides to classroom practice have been viewed and downloaded over 2.7 million times by teachers in more than 180 countries.

All Mike's resources can be downloaded for free at www.tes.co.uk/mikegershon

The TES (Times Educational Supplement) website is a wonderful platform providing user-generated content for teachers, by teachers. It is an online community of professionals which reaches into the heart of classrooms across the globe, bringing great resources to teachers and learners on every continent of the planet.

Having seen how his fellow professionals responded to his resources, Mike knew he had to go that one step further and provide book-length material that could help teaching and learning in classrooms throughout the world. And so, thanks in no small part to the fantastic platform provided by the TES, the 'How to...' series was born.

For more information on Mike, his books, training and consultancy, other writing and resources, visit www.mikegershon.com

Acknowledgements

First and foremost I must thank Jeremy Hayward, who taught me to teach. He has been a major influence and he is, without doubt, the best teacher I know. Thanks also to the many great teachers I have had over the years, specifically Judith Schofield, Richard Murgatroyd, Simon Mason, Cath Nealon, Andrew Gilliland, Graham Ferguson, and Simon Ditchfield. I must also thank all the wonderful teachers I have worked with and learnt from at Central Foundation Girls' School, Nower Hill High School, Pimlico Academy and King Edward VI School, Bury St. Edmunds. Special mention must go to the Social Sciences team at Pimlico, to Jon Mason and to James Wright. Of course, I cannot fail to thank all the fantastic students I have had the pleasure of teaching – particularly all the members of HC and HD at Pimlico. In addition, I am greatly indebted to the people I trained with at the IOE and, in particular, to Erin, Liam, Anna and Rahwa. Finally, thanks to my mum for her unfailing support over the years and her wonderful example.

I have picked up many of the activities, strategies and techniques in this book from the countless wonderful people I have worked with, however, any errors or omissions remain my own.

Other Works from the Same Author

Available to buy now on Amazon:

How to use Differentiation in the Classroom: The Complete Guide

How to use Assessment for Learning in the Classroom: The Complete Guide

How to use Questioning in the Classroom: The Complete Guide

How to use Discussion in the Classroom: The Complete Guide

How to Teach EAL Students in the Classroom: The Complete Guide

More Secondary Starters and Plenaries

Secondary Starters and Plenaries: History

Teach Now! History: Becoming a Great History Teacher

The Growth Mindset Pocketbook (with Professor Barry Hymer)

Also available to buy now on Amazon, the entire 'Quick 50' Series:

50 Quick and Brilliant Teaching Ideas

50 Quick and Brilliant Teaching Techniques

50 Quick and Easy Lesson Activities

50 Quick Ways to Help Your Students Secure A and B Grades at GCSE

50 Quick Ways to Help Your Students Think, Learn, and Use Their Brains Brilliantly

50 Quick Ways to Motivate and Engage Your Students

50 Quick Ways to Outstanding Teaching

50 Quick Ways to Perfect Behaviour Management

50 Quick and Brilliant Teaching Games

50 Quick and Easy Ways to Outstanding Group Work

50 Quick and Easy Ways to Prepare for Ofsted

50 Quick and Easy Ways Leaders can Prepare for Ofsted

Table of Contents

Chapter One – Introduction

Welcome to *How to Use Questioning in the Classroom*. Contained within are a wealth of practical ideas, activities and techniques which teachers can pick up and begin using immediately, no matter what age group they teach, or what area of the curriculum they specialise in.

It is a book which will help you to improve your own classroom practice, as well as the learning experience of your students.

Everything has been written with the busy teacher in mind. The strategies, techniques and activities which follow are all ready-to-use and take account of the practicalities of day-to-day teaching.

In addition, there are over 1200 generic, classroom-ready questions which you can adapt to fit whatever topic you are teaching.

This is a book which will help you to be a brilliant teacher.

It is a book which will help you to raise achievement.

It is a book that will help you to make your classroom an engaging, motivational environment in which learning and critical thinking are at the top of everyone's agenda.

The book is divided up as follows:

Section One – Questions: Strategies, Activities and Techniques

Chapter Two – An introduction to the nature of questions

Chapter Three – Fifteen ready-to-use questioning strategies and techniques

Chapter Four – Twenty ready-to-use questioning activities

Section Two – Exemplar Questions

Chapter Five – Introduction to the exemplar questions

Chapter Six – Comprehension Questions

Chapter Seven – Application Questions

Chapter Eight – Analysis Questions

Chapter Nine – Synthesis Questions

Chapter Ten – Evaluation Questions

Chapter Eleven – Philosophical Questions covering each area of the curriculum

Chapter Twelve – Plenary Questions

Chapter Thirteen – Example of Questions around a Theme

Chapter Fourteen – Conclusion

Chapter two analyses the nature of questions. It provides a theoretical underpinning for all that follows. If you prefer to focus on that which is immediately practical, you can skip the chapter and head straight to chapters three and four. These contain a wide range of strategies, activities and techniques which you can put into practice directly. All are clearly explained in the context of classroom teaching.

Section two presents more than 1200 ready-made questions which you can adapt to fit into any lesson. In these questions, the letter 'X' is used to represent whatever you want the question to be about.

So, for example:

'How might X be different in the future?'

Could become:

'How might democracy be different in the future?'

'How might worship be different in the future?'

'How might our school be different in the future?'

And so on.

By presenting the questions in this way, I have ensured that you can make use of them no matter what topic you are teaching.

Chapters six to ten cover questions connected to Bloom's Taxonomy of Educational Objectives.

Chapter eleven provides philosophical questions connected to each subject on the curriculum.

Chapter twelve provides ninety plenary questions which can be used in any lesson, regardless of what content has been covered.

Chapter thirteen gives an example of how to create a set of questions around a theme.

Chapter fourteen offers a brief conclusion.

Of course, it is up to you how you use this book. My own suggestion is to see it as a compendium of ideas which can be taken on and embedded in your own pedagogy or used to plan engaging, inspiring and enjoyable lessons. However you choose to use it, I am sure that it will bring significant benefits to your professional practice and also to the learning experience of your students.

Chapter Two - What Is a Question?

In this chapter we will analyse the nature of questions. This will provide a theoretical underpinning to the practical activities, strategies and techniques, together with the sample questions, which are to follow.

If you prefer to focus on that which is of immediate use in the classroom, you can skip ahead to chapter three.

To begin, we can highlight a number of traits those things classified as questions share:

  i.   In writing, the presence of a question mark. In speech, a specific inflection.
  ii.   The purpose of eliciting information in the form of a response.
  iii. The use of one or more directional words. That is, words which direct the respondent in how they ought to frame their response.
  iv.   The undertone of command (think of the phrase, 'a question that demands an answer').
  v.   The desire for reciprocity.

These traits can be said to be present in most questions (rhetorical questions are, of course, a special case). Let us explore each in turn so as understand them a little better.

Consider this:

1.1) What is a question

1.2) What is a question?

2.1) How are you

2.2) How are you?

3.1) Where might be the best place to position a wind turbine

3.2) Where might be the best place to position a wind turbine?

The question mark has the primary function of indicating that the text which precedes it ought to be treated as a question. In cases **1.1**, **2.1** and **3.1** it is natural for us to assume that the collection of words is indeed a question. This demonstrates how accustomed we are to the general form which questions take. It also demonstrates that we are able to use our knowledge of questions to make inferences about items which appear to have most of the elements of a question, though not all of them.

Equally, if we were to say statements **1.1**, **2.1** and **3.1** to someone, it is likely they would assume that we were asking them a question. We would probably find it difficult to say the statements without adding an inflection to indicate the fact that they are questions. The listener would probably think it odd that something which sounds like a question has not been clearly signalled as such.

There are two conventions then, one written and one spoken, which act as signals to the audience that a question has been asked. The functions of these are as follows:

i.   To minimise ambiguity.
ii.   To (in so doing) define that which has been said or written as a question.
iii. To close a sentence (in lieu of a full stop).

iv. To signify command (a question is asked, it is not said. Consider the difference in the connotations of those two words).

v. Through the combination of points i-iv, to indicate the desire for reciprocity.

Imagine we are interacting with a very young child, one who has not yet developed language. It would be quite natural for us to ask this child questions: 'Who's a good boy then?' 'What is it? What's up sweetie?' 'Who likes a tickle? Is it you?' These questions do not draw a response in language – other than from the speaker, who might choose to answer themselves – but they may draw a physical reply of some sort. If so, this is not a response to the question as a user of language would respond, but a response to stimulation; the brute information of the senses, before any coatings of culture (and therefore of meaning) have been layered on top.

The act of asking questions of another being who cannot possibly respond in kind throws up a number of interesting points. First, it suggests the centrality of questioning in our use of language. Second, it points to the importance of the child acquiring an understanding of the practice of question-asking during their development. Third, it intimates the reciprocal nature of our experience, both outside and inside of language. We will look at this final point in more detail.

Language is a tool which allows humans to communicate with one another. Words signify things. As do collections of words. Speaker and listener understand (perhaps exactly, perhaps loosely) what these significations are. If I say to you 'I saw a dog yesterday', you know that:

'I' is a term used to refer to the self. In this case the self is the speaker in question – Mike Gershon.

'Saw' is the past tense of 'see', meaning to take in visually the sight of something.

'A dog' means that there was one thing of that class which we refer to as dogs (the class being defined by a series of aspects which are common and which have to be found in something for it to be specified as belonging to that class).

'Yesterday' means the day before today (today meaning the present period of time, between the hours of 00.00AM and 11.59PM, which we are in – that itself being defined by the mechanical measure of time we have put in place through the use of clocks. Yesterday meaning the same as today except one full cycle of the clock previous).

We could further analyse each of the words in order to reveal that an understanding of the simple sentence I spoke to you actually relies upon and contains an even greater range of knowledge. What we have shown is sufficient to make the point however. That being, that language is a shared tool which exists independently of any one individual human and which acts as a means to share that which is inside of us (thoughts, sensations and so on) – this includes our experience of that which is outside of us (for example: I did not share with you the dog itself, but my experience of having seen the dog).

Getting back to the fact of asking questions of a child who cannot respond, we can see that the reciprocal aspect of questioning – which is clearly bound up with the nature of language as we have just briefly outlined – is to the fore.

The parent is interacting with their child. They are including them in the language community. They are modelling for them what the speaking of language is. This is not just through the words though – it is also through the functions and conventions of how those words are put together.

Questions then, are by their nature reciprocal. Language is a bridge between the separate minds we all possess. Questions play a key part in language. One of their main functions is to provide a starting point for the building of a bridge (the answer is the end point. There may be many bridges, millions in fact; there is, after all, so much we might connect).

We have considered briefly points (i) and (v). Let us now think about point (ii) – that questions are asked in order to elicit responses.

Based on what has been said so far, we are working under the assumption that when a question is asked it is done so with the expectation of reciprocity and that it is known as a question through the use of a commonly understood convention.

We can deduce from these premises that questions will be asked with the intention of evoking a response. If all questions are imbued with a sense of reciprocity, and if all collections of words which are questions are signified by a convention, then inevitably the onus is placed on the audience to offer some kind of response. This need not be spoken or written – it could simply be thought. Consider for example, when one reads a textbook containing questions. The author has clearly intended that the reader should take account of these, though it is likely they will do so in their mind, rather than through speech.

The traits of reciprocity and response-elicitation are closely linked. Both point to the fact that questions reach out to other minds. The difference, however, is that reciprocity refers to the general nature of questions, and response-elicitation refers to the specific act that a questioner is seeking to induce. Let us look at some examples in order to make this clearer:

1. What did you buy today?
2. How much are these?
3. I'm worried about Johnny, what do you think we should do?

In case (1), the questioner is seeking to elicit very specific information. They want to bridge the gap between their own mind and the mind of the person they are speaking to regarding what has been bought. This may be for a number of reasons, for example:

- They may be worried about money.
- They may be interested or may want to give the appearance of being interested.
- They may want to create an opportunity to talk about something they themselves have bought.

The list of motives we could ascribe to such a question is long. Suffice to say, whatever the motive, there is contained within the question a general sense of reciprocity: 'I am asking this. I am signalling that it is something that is being asked through my use of the convention. Therefore, I am showing that I want to create something with you – a conversation, an exchange, an airing of views or whatever.' At the same time, the particular elements of the question combine to request a response; in this case, what that is will probably prove to be quite specific.

Here, we will do well to connect point (iii). That is, the use of directional words – words which give the person being questioned an idea of what sort of a response is being requested. Let us exemplify this, as well as continuing to distinguish between reciprocity and response-elicitation, by looking at case (2).

'How much are these?' is a statement which is likely to be used in a shop or market. It is underpinned by a sense of reciprocity – the questioner has not just picked up the item and placed it in front of the seller. Nor have they gesticulated at it while pointing at their wallet. Having said that, you may be prepared to argue that the nature of the question militates against reciprocity; the questioner is seeking a highly specific response; they are after a small piece of information which they can use in conjunction with other things they know about or feel toward the item in question. Any question is only one half of a bridge though. In this case, it is still open to the person being asked the question to take it as an opportunity to talk at length, ask another question or provide a narrative which explains the price which is being requested. This gives us a sense of how reciprocity and response-elicitation exist at one and the same time. It also further supports the contention that they share some aspects as well as having points of difference.

Now let us turn to the idea of directional words. 'How much are these?' has the function of response-elicitation (think how put out the person would be if the shopkeeper ignored them) and the inherent sense of reciprocity. The scope of these two aspects is limited by the structure of the question itself. There are two parts: 'How much' and 'are these'. We analyse them thus:

- **'How much...'** indicates to the person being questioned that a specific piece of information is being requested. It signals that this information ought to be numerical or, at the very least, in reference to the number system (for example: a lot). The 'how' directs the listener through negation (it is not who, what, when, why or where) and through indication ('how' suggests that one ought to specify from within a range of possible options). The 'much' indicates what range of possibilities the 'how' is referring to in its request for specification. Therefore, we know that we are to specify from the range of numbers or terms which signify numerical degree.

- **'...are these'** indicates that the specific quantitative measure is in relation to an object which is present (and, we might infer, this object is being physically indicated by the speaker in such a way that the listener is made aware of to what they are referring). The 'are' points to the numerical degree being that which is the case at the present moment in time. The 'these' indicates the object to which the preceding words are referring – that thing in the world about which the question is being asked; the items about which the questioner would like to elicit information.

Let us now think about how the words might direct the response of the person to whom the question is being posed.

First, the use of 'how much' pushes any response in a certain direction. True, the shopkeeper could ignore this and say something like: 'they are beautiful, aren't they?' But this is less likely than them responding in accordance with the significations conjured up by the two words. Second, the term 'are these' clearly directs the shopkeeper's attention to certain items about which the person wants to know. They are unlikely to respond by talking about something completely different.

We have then, two points of which we need to be aware:

1. Questions may contain individual words or collections of words which indicate a specific type of response, a specific area in which a response ought to sit, or a style of responding which ought to be adopted. This is exemplified above through the case of 'How much...'

2. Questions may contain individual words or collections of words which indicate what the question is about. This is exemplified above through the case of '...are these'.

It is fair to say that most questions, perhaps all questions, will contain these two elements. The latter is not of great importance – all sentences need to be about something. If we ask a question it will only function correctly if the listener understands what it is we are asking about. The former, on the other hand, is very important. In order to illustrate why, let us consider the case as a matter of form versus content.

Here is a question:

'How big is X?'

This question could be asked innumerable times with X being replaced on each occasion by a different word:

- How big is France?
- How big is a fox?
- How big is a football?
- How big is Barry?

- How big is reggae music?

Throughout, the form of the question remains the same while the content changes. Such changes allow us to find out information of the type indicated by 'how big is...' concerning all manner of different things. What must be noted though, is that the form of the answers is likely to be roughly the same in each case. It will vary to some degree due to the different means of measurement we use for the various items. But it is likely to hold to a similar style in each case. This is because, generally, the form of the question has greater power in directing the response than the content of the question.

This is a really important point for us to remember when we are asking questions in the classroom. It bears repeating:

Generally, the form of a question has greater power in directing responses than the content of the question.

Let us make a brief diversion to the courtroom to reinforce this point.

When a barrister examines or cross-examines a witness, the content of their questions is important. It is this which determines which areas of the case the witness is to speak about. It is the form of their questions, however, which exerts far greater power.

A really good barrister will control the witness (almost imperceptibly) by asking questions in such a way as to help make their own client's case. They will do this, for example, by asking a series of questions which can only be answered with short, highly specific responses. Often this will be as specific as 'yes' or 'no'. The point will not be to create testimony which is false. Rather, it will be to direct the witness so that what they say shows the barrister's client's case in the best light possible.

If the barrister stood up and said to the witness, 'Tell me, sir, what happened?' they could receive all manner of responses – many of which might prove highly detrimental to their client's case (for example, if the witness interpreted something differently from someone else). This is because the question is formed in such a way as to give the person being questioned a license to go in whatever direction they choose.

Here is an example which demonstrates what we are arguing:

Barrister: What is your name?

Witness: John Smith?

B: Where do you live?

W: 3, Hampton Gardens

B: Do you know the defendant?

W: Yes

B: Do you know the defendant through work or through some other way?

W: Through work

B: Do you work with the defendant at Hatton's carpets?

W: Yes

B: How long have you worked at Hatton's Carpets?

W: One year

B: Do you know how long the defendant has worked at Hatton's Carpets?

W: Yes

B: Can you tell us please, how long the defendant has worked at Hatton's Carpets?

W: One year – he started the same day as I did.

B: Did you receive training when you began working at Hatton's?

W: Yes

B: Did this include health and safety training?

W: Yes

B: Did the health and safety training extend to use of the industrial carpet cleaner?

W: No, it did not.

B: Did the training cover the use of industrial strength chemicals?

W: No.

B: Did the defendant receive the same training as you?

W: Yes

B: How do you know?

W: Because he was with me at all the sessions

B: No further questions

In this example, the barrister keeps the witness on a short leash. The form of the questions means that only certain responses are permissible (by permissible, we mean as regards the rules of language which we expect one another to follow in everyday life as well as those which people are expected to follow in the courtroom). The barrister was not leading the witness (as in: 'The training didn't cover industrial strength chemicals, did it?'), they were directing them. This was done through the form of each specific question and through the overall structure of the questioning.

I will present one more example in order to demonstrate the importance of form in directing responses:

What is democracy?

What might democracy be?

To this, we will return. For the moment, however, let us use the third of our questions to explore point (iv) – the undertone of command. The question was as follows: 'I'm worried about Johnny, what do you think we should do?'

Reciprocity and response-elicitation are both present here. The latter in the sense that the speaker wants to know the thoughts of the other person, the former in what seems quite a strong sense – that of Johnny being a subject of shared concern.

At the same time, the question is commanding the listener to respond. The speaker is using language in order to induce something in someone else. The question is an act in the way that a straight statement is not. For example:

I like fish

Do you like fish?

The first collection of words is an expression of what one thinks; the second collection of words is requesting someone else's thoughts on the matter of fish. In this sense, questions command a listener to respond. There are varying degrees of command, none of which guarantee a response, but all of which make the demand.

It is best to think of these degrees as continuous rather than discrete. This leads us to a continuum model in which questions range from those containing a low level of command to those containing a high level of command. Here is a demonstration of this point:

What are your thoughts on fish?

What do you think about fish?

What do you know about fish?

What, precisely, do you know about fish?

Do you want fish tonight or not?

Have you got a problem with me eating fish in front of you?

Why are you bringing a fish into this house at this hour?

Why are you bringing a fish into this house at this hour, while wearing that smug look on your face?

You will notice that the higher levels of command correlate with a desire to know more specific information. In the last case, the question is being wielded almost as a weapon, with the speaker demanding a response which, in itself, has been heavily circumscribed by the manner of the question.

Thinking back to our example of the barrister, we may also define their questions as containing a high level of command. As with the questions at the end of the above list, those were being used with the intention of building bridges between minds which were based very much on the questioner's own terms.

It is important to add that the level of command contained in a question is not exclusive to the wording. In speech, the intonation, body language and gesture which accompany the asking of questions also play a significant role.

What are the implications of this for the classroom?

Having considered what questions are we shall now take a step from the general to the specific and look at what implications our analysis holds for classroom practice. In order to make this clear and succinct, I will address each of the five traits in turn.

i) **In writing, the presence of a question mark. In speech, a specific inflection.**

In order for students to understand that we are asking a question, we must use the appropriate convention. It is unlikely that any issue will arise regarding the written word. On occasion, it may be the case that a student does not interpret an inflection as the teacher intended them to do. This is simply dealt with by repeating the question and, if necessary, stressing the intonation.

i.   The purpose of eliciting responses.

It is of vital importance to consider what type of responses we want from students. Teachers need to ask themselves why they are asking a question. If this is not done, the effectiveness of questioning will diminish.

There are many types of information we might want to elicit in the classroom. This includes:

- Information about what students already know.
- Information concerning what students can recall.
- Information connected to what students understand.
- Information related to what students have heard, read or watched.
- Information which is diagnostic.
- Information which is a summary of what has been learnt.
- Information which reveals a process.
- Information which provides insight into opinions or beliefs.
- Information which demonstrates a skill (for example, reasoning).
- Information which can be assessed.
- Information that has been used.
- Information which reveals an interpretation.

The list – which could go on further – indicates the wide range of options which can inform a teacher's use of questioning.

By considering in advance the purpose of your questioning, three benefits are likely to accrue:

1. You will create and ask questions which are predicated on your purpose. This will result in you getting the information you want.
2. You will be able to use questioning in order to further student learning. This is because you will be creating interactions which are purposeful and which are tied to the aims of your teaching.
3. You will save time. This is because you won't have to think 'in the moment' about what it is you want to know. Having to do this usually results in longer, less focussed periods of questioning in which it is not clear to teacher or students what precisely is going on or why.

So, the fact that questions elicit responses means that teachers should think about what responses they would like and what exactly they are using questioning for.

It should be noted here that I am not suggesting the only questions which should be asked are those which will require a highly specific response. Rather, that the teacher should have an idea of what type of responses they want and why they want them. For example, in a Citizenship lesson one might what reasoned responses which propose arguments about a certain point. In terms of content that is vague, but in terms of form it is highly specific.

ii.   **The use of one or more directional words. That is, words which direct the respondent in how they ought to frame their response.**

Teachers need to be careful how they structure their questions and the extent to which they direct their students. Earlier on we used the following example:

What is democracy?

What might democracy be?

In the first case, the use of 'what is...' causes the respondent to assume that a specific answer exists and that this is what must be sought. The word 'what' indicates the request of information. The word 'is' indicates that the subject of the sentence is a specific thing definable at the present time. The combination of 'what' and 'is' therefore works to create a sense in the respondent's mind that the range of possible answers has been severely delimited. The request for information has been circumscribed. It is a request for a specific answer.

In the second case, the concern with the present nature of the subject remains (indicated through the use of the word 'be'), but this is achieved without any delimitation. The reason for this is the use of the word 'might'. This word signifies the *possibility* of something being true. In the question 'what might democracy be?' it renders democracy something about which there are many possibilities. Due to the nature of a question, this in turn lends itself to the idea that there are a range of possible answers, all of which could be accepted by the questioner.

This example serves to demonstrate how the wording of a question can have a significant impact on how students respond. In addition, it can have a major impact on what information the teacher is able to elicit. If a teacher continually asks questions of the first type, it is unlikely that they will:

- Reveal much about student understanding
- Encourage discussion
- Encourage reasoning

- Allow students to learn by making mistakes
- Give students the opportunity to explore ideas

It may not always be possible to ask questions of the second type – and in some cases in may not be preferable for one reason or another – but it is vitally important that teachers are always aware of how their use of directional words can limit the answers their students feel able to give. If you take one thing away from this section, let it be this:

Questions contain the seeds of their own answers. Think carefully about what you want to grow.

iii. The undertone of command (think of the phrase, 'a question that demands an answer').

When teachers ask questions they should give consideration to the level of command they want their questions to contain, and why it is that they would like to use that particular level of command. One of the skills which you develop over time is a sense of what fits – what is apt – in various settings. It may be that certain classes or topics make quite clear demands in relation to the level of command, whereas others do not offer such help – leaving it up to the teacher to feel their way. Here are two examples of situations where the level of command is decided for the teacher.

Imagine you have a difficult class who are liable to behave poorly if not kept on a tight rein. This may lead you to ask questions which have a high level of command. In so doing, you are keeping your students under close control and not allowing any leeway which might be taken advantage of for disruptive ends. It could be that some of the questions you ask are made to contain a higher level of command than the wording suggests because of how you go about asking them. It might also be that you use more written questions than spoken ones. Part of the high level of command will thus come from the fact that you are making clear the necessity of written responses.

Imagine now that you are teaching a sensitive topic such as bereavement. It is likely that the subject matter would direct you to ask questions containing a low level of command. This is because anything else would be inappropriate for the context. Questions with a high level of command would create an atmosphere not conducive to the sharing of opinions, beliefs and feelings. In addition, they would stymie the development of discussion. This is primarily because such a topic requires the gentle teasing out of answers and responses.

These two examples are indicative of the many situations where outside factors will limit the options available to the teacher regarding levels of command. At other times, it is best if the teacher considers the purpose(s) of their questioning and then attempts to tally that with level of command which they think is appropriate.

It is also important to note that various levels can be used throughout a lesson. In addition, a teacher can alter the level they are using mid-question, or during the course of a series of questions, in response to the reactions coming from students.

It also possible to repeat or rephrase a question so that it contains a different level of command – the decision to do so having been based on the response (or lack of response) engendered by the original question.

iv.   The desire for reciprocity.

Asking questions in a classroom is a way of bridging the gap between minds. By asking questions and by thinking carefully about what questions to ask, the teacher is able to cultivate an atmosphere of reciprocity in which knowledge and understanding are developed in cooperation, rather than in a manner which is didactic.

All the other elements we have looked at play a part in how the desire for reciprocity is manifested. In one sense, what is at issue here is the ethos or culture the teacher seeks to create through their use of questioning. It may be that a satisfactory character to your questioning develops organically, or it may be that you need to work actively in order to achieve it.

The best advice I can give you is that repetition is the most effective tool at your disposal. If you continue to ask questions in such a way as to indicate a positive sense of reciprocity then, eventually, a concomitant atmosphere is likely to come about. On the other hand, if your questioning lacks consistency than it will be harder for students to understand how it is they are to act in relation to it. Therefore, they will be less likely to exhibit the attitude you are seeking from them.

Conclusion

This introductory chapter has sought to provide some theoretical insight. The reasons for this are twofold. First, it is hoped that through reading what has gone before you will have developed a more critical attitude toward questioning, one which sees the practice analytically and allows you to conceive of the various ways in which it might affect what goes on in your classroom.

Second, the points made in this chapter underpin and inform the practical material which is to follow. By placing this chapter first I have intended that you will be able to make use of the strategies, techniques, activities and example questions with a deeper understanding of their rationale than might otherwise have been the case. Here is a summary of the key points:

- A collection of traits are shared by nearly all questions.
- Questions direct the person being questioned, contain a level of command, and aim to elicit a response.
- Questions help bridge the gap between minds.
- Questions promote reciprocity.
- Generally, the form of a question has greater power in directing responses than the content of the question.
- Questions contain the seeds of their own answers. Therefore, you should think carefully about what you want to grow.

Chapter Three – Strategies and Techniques

In this chapter we will look at fifteen different strategies and techniques which will help you to use questioning more effectively in the classroom.

1. Making Knowledge Provisional

Here are some beliefs that, in various societies and at various times, have held sway:

- The Earth is flat.
- Celestial bodies revolve around the Earth, which is stationary.
- The human body is filled with four basic substances (yellow bile, black bile, blood and phlegm). When these are out of balance, people's health and temperament deteriorates.
- All swans are white.
- Phlogiston is a fire-like element which is released during combustion.

All of these beliefs have been subsequently disproved. Yet, at one time – and in some cases for extremely long periods – they were held by large numbers of people. In turn, those people's thinking and behaviour was influenced, directed and informed by what we now recognise to be erroneous beliefs. In some cases, information which refuted the beliefs was met with derision, disdain or worse. Justifications and proofs were presented which claimed to explain why the beliefs were true. Counter-proposals received short shrift.

And yet, here we are, in a position to know that each of these theories is false. Our study of astronomy and physics has shown us that the Earth is a sphere, that it moves through space orbiting the sun and that the moon is the only celestial body which revolves around it.

Developments in medicine have demonstrated that the body is not filled with four basic substances. Many different causes have been identified which explain the presence or development of diseases, illnesses and afflictions.

It has been shown through observation that some swans are black.

Phlogiston does not exist. Combustion involves the burning of oxygen; plenty of tests have been developed to prove this. These can be replicated by different people in different parts of the world.

We can draw two points from this. First, human understanding changes over time. In addition, through the use of various tools – including writing, observation, scientific method and numeracy – it can be said that human understanding of the world has developed. Second, it is through the exercising of critical faculties that individuals have come to develop alternative theories and explanations to those which are taken for granted.

As teachers, we want to develop critical mind-sets in the classroom. One way in which to do this is to present knowledge as being provisional rather than fixed. This can be achieved through questioning.

The use of the word 'might' – as discussed in the introduction – is a simple way of achieving this. If we alter a question so that it presents an idea or process as open to a variety of possible explanations, then we are promoting the use of reason, analysis and critical thinking in the classroom.

Instead of asking students to guess the right answer which the teacher knows and wants to impart, we are helping pupils to arrive at a reasoned answer which is built on careful thinking and discussion.

What is democracy?

What might democracy be?

The latter question will cause students to reason, analyse, assess and examine. The former cannot provide such a guarantee. Given information, evidence and examples by the teacher, pupils will be able to arrive individually and as a group at an answer (or a collection of answers) which are predicated on critical thinking.

Two further benefits accrue from making knowledge provisional. First, the teacher is able to elicit detailed information from students concerning what they think and why they think it. This is of much greater use than information likely to be elicited by a non-provisional question. It means that the teacher can get an insight into students' thinking. They can then use this to adjust their teaching including, for example, by asking further questions, offering counter-examples or by seeking justifications for that which has been said.

The second benefit is that theories, answers and ideas are tested in a critical crucible – one in which logic, evidence, examples and reasoning must be utilised in order for something to stand. Making knowledge provisional means placing it in reference to the set of criteria which has developed since the Enlightenment and which underpins what we are prepared to accept as true (or as near to true as we can know at present). Questioning in this way thus trains students to think critically – both through making specific response-demands and by subjecting their responses to further analysis and evaluation.

Here are two brief exchanges to illustrate what is being argued:

Teacher: What is democracy?

Student: Is it a type of political system?

Teacher: Yes. Well done.

Teacher: What might democracy be?

Student: Democracy might be something which we should aspire to.

Teacher: What makes you think that?

Student: Well, it is something which you hear a lot about in newspapers and on television and people tend to talk about it as a good thing.

Teacher: What might make people see it as a good thing?

Student: Well, I know that democracy involves people voting on things. So, perhaps, people think voting on things is good.

Teacher: Why do you think it might be good to vote on things?

The latter example would be concluded, eventually, with a request for a formal definition of democracy. That definition would be informed by a lengthy discourse, one in which the teacher has had an opportunity to probe the knowledge and understanding of their students.

In conclusion, there is a great deal to be gained from making knowledge provisional. It can be achieved through reshaping traditional questions. Other key words to use include 'may', 'could' and 'would'. You might also like to use questions stems such as: 'can you think of some different possibilities (regarding X)?' or 'What different answers might be possible (regarding X)?'

2. Using Questions to frame Lessons or Activities

The pursuit of knowledge is built on the asking of questions. The development of understanding, the expression of beauty and the search for meaning are predicated on questions. Questions formulate – sometimes baldly, sometimes badly, sometimes in a manner which transforms thinking beyond all recognition – the curiosity which shapes us as human beings; that inward urge to know, to understand and to come to terms with.

A question is like an arrow which points towards the future. It directs us to an end. It informs the means by which we will seek to act or think. These aspects of questioning can be harnessed for use in the classroom. Consider the following examples:

1.1 Lesson Title: The effect of pollution on cities

1.2 Lesson Title: If cities breathe, do their lungs get clogged?

2.1 Activity Title: Essay Writing

2.2 Activity Title: Why write essays?

Questions can be used to frame lessons or individual activities. In so doing, the teacher is invoking a sense of enquiry with which to direct and inspire their students. In **1.1**, there is the intimation that we will be working through information and ideas connected to the title. In **1.2**, there is the indication that we will be trying to answer the question. The information and ideas we work through will be harnessed in order for us to attempt to reach a conclusion. There is a greater sense of purpose and endeavour in the second formulation. The sentence is transformed from passive to active.

In **2.1** and **2.2**, the activity title journeys from being a straight indication of what content is likely to follow to a question which aims to get at the very core of the issue. Both will result in students learning about essay writing. Both might even contain identical content. The latter, however, will frame it around an active analysis – at the end of the lesson students will be able to judge their success by considering whether or not they can answer the question.

We might like to conceive of this idea of using questions to frame lessons and activities as a retreat from the notion of a title. The latter is a name or a descriptive heading. Something which signals what is to come but is, of itself in the classroom, essentially procedural. The former is not a title – it is a question; a question in place of a title; a question replacing a title.

Questions command a response and indicate reciprocity. Questions framed in the manner of **1.2** and **2.2** point to something which is at issue, which needs to be resolved, investigated, examined or assessed. They give a lesson or an activity a clear purpose beyond the underlying point of 'being at school to learn'. They provide something which the whole class – teacher included – can work towards. That is, the finding of some sort of answer.

In addition, the replacing of a title with a question can make it easier to delineate between different activities and different lessons. This is because a conclusion can be signalled through discussion of what an appropriate answer might be (or through writing down appropriate answers). This is like drawing the enquiry to a close. It provides an endpoint which is clear, succinct and meaningful.

3. How to Encourage Responses

In the classroom you can find yourself in the frustrating position of asking a question and getting no response (and the question is not meant to be rhetorical!). The feeling derives from the traits of questions we explored in the introduction and, in particular, those concerning the commanding of a response and the wider sense of reciprocity.

When we ask a question to a student, we expect a response. If we did not then there would be no point in asking a question (unless it was rhetorical). There are a number of reasons why students might not respond to our questions. These include:

- They do not know the answer
- They do not feel confident
- They do not understand the question
- They have not listened to the question
- They feel social pressure which prevents them from answering
- They are bored
- They are seeking to undermine the teacher
- They are seeking to be disruptive
- They do not feel sufficiently safe or comfortable to share their thoughts
- They fear getting the answer wrong

Many reasons exist as to why students might not answer a question. To try and deal with each of these would take an age. Better instead to pre-empt them. The way to do this is by structuring your questioning so that you minimise the potential for any of the reasons to come into play. Here are five approaches you might like to use:

- Avoid questions that require a single, direct answer, such as: 'What is the capital of Mongolia?' Of course, there will be times when such questions are useful – and times when they are unavoidable – but, in general, questions like these will discourage many students from responding. This is because they will be thinking something along the lines of: 'There is one right answer to this and I don't want to be seen to get it wrong.'

- Use questions that invite students to talk about what they think, such as: 'What do you know about Mongolia?' When it comes to questions of this type, the stakes are much lower. It is not a question of there being one right answer and a whole host of others which are wrong. Rather, it is about students sharing their thoughts with the teacher and with the class.

- Ask students to talk to their partner first. By giving time for students to discuss in pairs, you alleviate two key problems: the social awkwardness of being the first person to speak and the numerical imbalance between teacher and students. If you stand in front of a class and ask a question – who is to answer? You are conceiving of the class as a unit because you are speaking to them all at the same time. They cannot answer as a unit though. Nor is it likely that one person will take it upon themselves to respond. And if they do – is that really what you want? One voice sharing their thoughts on behalf of all others? Asking students to discuss in pairs first means that everybody in the class will have a safe, easy environment in which to get to grips with the question and to share an answer.

- Give students thinking time. Ask a question and then...wait. By waiting you will be giving them time to think. This means that they will be able to analyse the question and consider what response to give. It can be easy to fall into the trap of asking a question and then demanding an immediate response. Another common ambush comes in the form of asking one question after another, in quick succession. Both scenarios frequently creep up on teachers without their realising. A good way to avoid them, and to ensure you give thinking time, is to ask a question and then say out loud to students: 'Thirty seconds thinking time.' Another option is to say the question and then to count silently to ten. Slowly. Once you have done this, a little bit of thinking time will have been made available.

- Encourage students to write something down. If you write something down then you free up space in your short-term memory. You are also in a better position to reflect on and analyse that which you thought than if you continue to hold the information in your mind. In addition, students can refer to their notes when they come to share their thoughts. You might use phrases such as these to direct your students: 'Note down some thoughts about the question.' 'Make some notes about your response to the question.' 'What might X be? Make a note of your thoughts.'

4. Oral and Written Questioning

It is important to be aware of some of the differences between oral questioning and written questioning. This is so that teachers can achieve the most effective outcomes when using both. In this section we will look at the two types of questioning in turn, drawing out what is unique to each.

Oral Questioning

Oral questions are accompanied by gesture, intonation and inflexion. All of these contain information which helps students to unpack and unpick what it is they are being asked. Further, when a teacher poses a question in speech, they can use these various cues to make their meaning clearer.

In these situations, meaning does not stop at the literal meaning of the question. It also extends to the meaning of the question in context. So, for example, one might ask a question to a class, with the tone of voice softening markedly towards the end of the sentence. This would be a contextual cue indicating that the class should quieten down and reflect individually on the question.

A second point to note concerning oral questions is that speech is immediately editable. If a teacher asks a question and receives a quizzical look from a student, they can respond by instantly restating, rephrasing or reshaping the question. The underlying point here is that speech, as a technology, lends itself to communication more simply and more immediately than writing does. This is in part because of our greater experience in using speech but it is also a function of the structure of speech as well.

The final point to note concerning oral questions is that they do not need to be as formal as written prose. The conventions which order writing do not order speech. The latter is more malleable, more open-ended and more contingent on the situation in which it is being used. Of course, writing is also malleable, open-ended and contingent, but not to the same extent and not in the same manner. As an example, compare a letter or email written by a friend with a conversation you had with that same friend. Even in written communication between two people who are close, there are likely to be a greater number of inhibitions at work than in a spoken communication.

As an aside, one of the reasons for this is because of the isolated position in which writing finds itself. It is accompanied by nothing other than itself, save for a possible image, diagram or graph of some kind. Scan back over what you have just read. It is simply words arranged on a page. The shape and structure of those words gives them meaning but there is nothing supplemental. If I spoke the same words to you, even if you could not see me, you would have more to go on. This is one of the reasons why writing must adhere to stricter conventions than speech.

By keeping to these conventions, writers are trying to ensure that ambiguity is minimised in the communication between their mind and the reader's mind. That this communication can occur over great distances and times makes this still more important (and we have not even touched on the issue of interpretation).

Written Questioning

Written questions are fixed. One of the great advantages of this is that they remain the same across time and space. Imagine the potential for error if examination questions were spoken by exam boards to schools and then by teachers to students.

A further advantage of fixed questions is that they can be continually referred to and do not need to be remembered. This means that they maintain their exact form for the entirety of their physical existence and that they do not take up space in a student's short-term memory. Accordingly, students who are working with written questions know that they have a stable point of reference. This means they can turn their minds completely to the answer they are being asked to formulate.

Much of the work students do in class, and even more of the work they do in examinations, involves responding to written questions. There are two points we need to be aware of as a result.

First, it is incumbent on teachers who have exam classes to give their students the opportunity to practise answering exam-style questions. This does not mean teaching to the test, but it does mean ensuring students are able to familiarise themselves with what it is they will be asked to do in any test they have to take.

If this does not happen, pupils may enter examinations and find themselves viewing questions through a prism of ambiguity. It will not necessarily be the case that the questions will be ambiguous (though they might be). Rather, it is that students will not have experienced these types of questions before and therefore may find themselves at a loss as to how to respond.

Second, all writing, however clear, still carries within it the potential of being interpreted. Consider the following:

The box is not to be used.

OK. The box is not to be used. What happens if I could use the box to save a life? Would I then be able to use it? Why exactly is the box not to be used? If someone I dislike begs me to help them by using the box, can I refuse on the grounds that it is clearly stated that the box is not to be used? Also, when is the box not to be used? Forever? If so, what then is the point of the box? And why is it the case that the box cannot be used for a certain period of time? Can things inside the box be used? How exactly are we defining 'used'? If I dance around the box and use it as a totem – but don't touch it or move it – does that count as me using the box? Should I throw the box away? That could hardly be said to be using it – and it would prevent other people from using it, therefore fulfilling the sentence's message.

All writing is open to interpretation. In the context of the classroom, there are two points to which this gives rise.

First, it is of benefit to all involved if written questions make clear what type of response is being requested. This is because it helps students to answer in the desired manner and it helps teachers to ensure they get the responses they want. If you collect in work and find that it does not match expectations, it is worthwhile spending a few minutes thinking about whether this was a result of the questions which you set.

Second, it is important to teach students how to interpret questions. This will ensure they can analyse those put in front of them and will lead to a generally higher standard of responses. There are many ways to approach the issue. One example is to teach students the meaning of command words such as 'assess' and 'outline'. Another is to spend time imagining different responses before assessing these in accordance with some success criteria. A further method involves looking at questions and mark-schemes at the same time.

5. Questions and Discussion

Discussion is a superb addition to any classroom. It gives students an opportunity to develop and interrogate ideas, arguments and theories. It allows pupils to learn from and with one another. It provides a space in which knowledge and understanding can be cultivated. It allows misconceptions to be aired and learnt from. It gives the teacher lots of opportunity to elicit information from their students, with this then being used to inform teaching. It fosters a sense of cooperation and shared endeavour. It helps create a sense of community in which learning is central. It develops the critical faculties.

Questions play a vital role in discussion. It is likely they will frame, order and direct what is talked about. In addition, they will be used by students and teacher alike once the discussion has got going. Let us look at these two aspects in turn.

If questions are used to frame, order and direct discussion it is worthwhile spending a little time playing around with a variety of formulations during the planning stages. This need not take long – a few minutes ought to suffice – but it will be of great benefit in the long-run. This is because the discussion which eventually ensues is likely to be better and, if it is not, you will have some alternative options available which you can try instead.

Here are some pointers on coming up with good discussion questions:

- Think big. It is easier to start from the big picture and home in on specifics than vice versa.
- Find something which is, or could be, at issue. This can then act as a focus point for your discussion – something which contributions can revolve around.
- Pitch your questions carefully. Ensure pupils will have sufficient knowledge and understanding to talk about them for a sustained period of time.
- Make your questions clear (or be ready to explain them).

- Imbue your question with purpose. Ask yourself what you want students to get out of the discussion. Develop your questions accordingly.

You and your students are likely to use a number of questions during the course of the discussion. Here are some techniques which will prove useful for the teacher:

- Prepare some questions in advance which you think will be of use.
- Have a range of question stems or exemplar questions to hand which can be tailored to the present topic. This book contains 1200 sample questions you might like to use.
- Adopt different roles and use these to inform the types of question you ask. These can include the Socratic roles of gadfly, stingray, midwife and ignoramus (see my book, 'How to use Discussion in the Classroom' for more information) or other roles such as interrogator, judge, clarifier or devil's advocate.
- Encourage students to ask questions of one another. For example, when a pupil has made an extended statement, ask the class what questions they might now ask that student.
- Use a randomised system to choose who is to answer a question. This could involve pulling names out of a hat, assigning numbers to all students and then drawing one out at random, or writing your students' names on lollipop sticks from which you then select ones at random. The advantage of using such a system is that it avoids bias in the selection of who is to answer. Therefore, it is more likely that the teacher will get a true picture of the whole class's thinking and learning.

6. Differentiating Questioning

Questioning can be used to differentiate. The simplest way to do this is to vary the difficulty level of the questions you ask. Here are three methods you might use for this:

Bloom's Taxonomy

Bloom's Taxonomy of Educational Objectives provides a hierarchy of the various types of thinking we ask students to do in school. It ranges from simple tasks which require limited mastery of the material to complex processes which require a high level of mastery if they are to be performed effectively.

The taxonomy runs as follows: Knowledge; Comprehension; Application; Analysis; Synthesis; Evaluation. Some researchers have suggested that the last two categories should be swapped over. For our purposes it does not really matter – we need only acknowledge that synthesis and evaluation occupy the two highest levels.

In the 'exemplar questions' section of this book, a wide range of questions are provided based on the five highest levels of the taxonomy (knowledge is excluded as it is the most basic). These can be used to differentiate questioning. It is likely that pupils will find the lower-level questions easier to answer than the higher-level questions.

If you are using oral questioning, you can use Bloom's Taxonomy to tailor your questions to the students with whom you are speaking. If you are using written questioning, you can provide a range of questions that gradually move up Bloom's Taxonomy.

This will allow all pupils to access the work as well as ensuring that those who are more able are challenged and stretched.

An alternative to using the exemplar questions provided in this book is to familiarise yourself with a range of key words which link to each category of Bloom's Taxonomy, and to then use these to create your own questions. This could be done before the lesson or during interactions with students. You might even keep a sheet of paper to hand (or put one on the wall) which contains a range of key words for each level of the taxonomy. Here is a list of words which you might use:

Knowledge: Arrange, Define, Describe, List, Match, Memorise, Name, Order and Recognise.

Comprehension: Classify, Complete, Establish, Explain, Express, Identify, Illustrate and Report.

Application: Apply, Calculate, Choose, Employ, Interpret, Operate, Sketch, Solve and Suggest.

Analysis: Analyse, Categorize, Contrast, Distinguish, Examine, Experiment and Investigate.

Synthesis: Combine, Construct, Create, Devise, Design, Formulate, Organise and Plan.

Evaluation: Argue, Assess, Critique, Defend, Evaluate, Judge, Justify, Rank and Review.

Concrete to Abstract

This method is similar to that described above, but sufficiently different to warrant a separate explanation. It is similar because it involves imagining that questions exist on a continuum. At one end of the continuum are simple questions which are easy to access. At the other end of the continuum are complex question which are harder to access. As you can see, this is akin to the hierarchy of levels found in Bloom's Taxonomy.

The method is different, however, because it involves a gradual transition from one type of thinking to another, as opposed to a specific delineation of skills. That transition is from concrete thinking to abstract thinking. Here is an example:

Most Concrete

How many ducks are in the pond?

What colour are the ducks?

How are the ducks behaving?

What relationships exist between the ducks?

What might be influencing the behaviour and relationships of the ducks?

Why might the ducks have come to be as they are?

Is all human life mirrored in the vagaries of ducks?

If ducks could speak, would we understand them?

Most Abstract

A strong argument could be made that every question in the list is important. A similar argument could also be made about the type of answers these questions are seeking to elicit. Using the concrete to abstract model is thus not about privileging abstract over concrete thinking. Rather, it involves acknowledging the importance of both while simultaneously understanding the increased complexity of abstract thinking.

In practice, the method provides the teacher with a framework from which they can operate when using questions. It is a framework that will allow them to differentiate in the same way as the use of Bloom's Taxonomy; they can ask different types of questions to different students and they can use a variety of types when constructing written questions.

Show Me, Tell Me, Convince Me

This method functions on the same premise as the two previously outlined – that a framework can be provided through which questions gradually increase in difficulty, and that this can be used as a means to differentiate questioning. It works as follows:

Show me: Use the phrase 'show me' as the command part of your question. You might ask a student to show you what they have done, to show you how they have learnt something, or to show you what something means. The use of the word 'show' indicates that this activity will involve a basic level of thinking. Often, it will be possible for the student to respond without having to put their own interpretation on the material or without having to move below the surface of that with which they are interacting.

Tell me: Using the phrase 'tell me' as the command part of your question means you are making greater demands on your students. You might ask pupils to tell you what they think about something, to tell you about the structure of something, or to tell you about the origins of something they have been studying. The use of the word 'tell' indicates that this activity will require a deeper level of thinking than was the case with the word 'show'. 'Telling' something can only be done effectively if one has spent time thinking about the item in question. This thinking ought to have led to the development of knowledge and understanding. If it has not, the telling is unlikely to make much sense or to contain much that is of interest.

Convince me: Using the phrase 'convince me' as the command part of your question will result in even greater demands being made of your students. You might ask pupils to convince you that they are right, to convince you that something is the case, or to convince you that a certain course of action should be taken. The use of the word 'convince' indicates that this activity will require complex thinking – thinking which is beyond the level of showing and telling. Convincing someone of something requires the speaker to have a certain degree of mastery over their material. They must both understand the material and understand how to present it such that it persuades the audience of the point at issue. If someone's case is found to be unconvincing, it means that we do not have reason to believe what they are saying. This will be due to a lack of insight regarding the material or a lack of skill in presenting it. We may, of course, not agree with them, but this has limited bearing on whether the case they present is a convincing one or not.

7. Using Questions to Change, Challenge, Probe and Provoke

We have already noted that questions do things; that they have more power than most statements; and that they cause people to act. Here we will look at four specific things that questions can do and that are of particular use in the classroom.

Questions that (can) Change Thinking

The sentence is qualified by the insertion of '(can)' because it would be remiss to suggest that any question has the power to change someone else's thinking. To assert otherwise would be to pre-determine the power of a string of text, taking no account of the individual to whom it is being asked. Given as how questions are by their nature reciprocal, we cannot conceive of them as acting unilaterally on a person's mind. They have the power to elicit a response – but this is still only a power conferred rather than an absolute power (someone could ignore the question or remain mute). Therefore, no question can, definitively, change someone else's thinking. Many questions, however, have the potential to do so.

In the classroom, opportunities will arise where a well-timed and well-conceived question can cause students to look differently at that which they think they know or understand. Here are two examples which demonstrate this:

Example One:

Student: There is no doubt in my mind that the sun will rise tomorrow. It has risen every other day I have been alive, so why shouldn't it rise tomorrow?

Teacher: What problems might arise if you used that same logic in all of your life? What are the consequences for your lack of doubt concerning whether the sun will rise?

Example Two:

Student: There is no way World War Two could have been avoided. Europe had to act to stop Hitler. It would not have been possible to avoid starting a war. Appeasement was clearly a failure and the only option left was to react militarily to what Germany was doing.

Teacher: You are suggesting that there was no way World War Two could have been avoided?

Student: Yes.

Teacher: And you are basing that on the fact that appeasement had failed, that Hitler had to be stopped and that military action was the only viable option?

Student: Yes.

Teacher: If the terms of the Treaty of Versailles had been different, would the war have happened?

It is good to look for opportunities such as these, where a well-placed and well-considered question can open up new vistas of thought for students. In these two examples, pupils are being invited down different paths by the teacher. The questions they are faced with shine a light on areas of thinking which their initial comments did not take into account. The questions are tools which the teacher is using to further learning.

Challenging Questions

We may interpret the word 'challenging' in two ways. First, in the sense of challenging what students have said; second, in the sense of challenging students to think differently. We will look at each of these approaches in turn.

Challenging what students have said involves asking them to justify, clarify or explain their comments. Here are some examples:

Student 1: The best thing about the holidays is getting a lie-in.

Teacher 1: Why is that the best thing about the holidays?

Student 2: I don't think so, no.

Teacher 2: Can you explain what you mean by that?

Student 3: If we have to choose then I'll go for red.

Teacher 3: Just to clarify, have you chosen red at random because you have to choose something, or have you chosen red because you genuinely think it is better than the other options?

The key point here is that the teachers' questions cause students to think more deeply about what they have said. There is an indication that what has been articulated is incomplete or in need of development. The questions invite pupils to do something further with their original statements.

Challenging students to think differently involves asking questions which are designed to push their thinking. In this sense, the 'differently' can be interpreted in the following ways:

- To think differently from how they have been thinking up to the present point in time.
- To think differently from how they usually think.
- To think differently about the material in question.
- To use different skills or processes in order to consider the material in question from an alternative perspective.
- To think in a manner beyond that which has been encouraged up to the present point in time.

Questions which exemplify these categories can come in a range of different forms. Here are a collection of examples, some of which could be attributed to one of the categories, some of which could fit into multiple categories:

- How might your answer be different if democracy no longer existed?
- What assumptions or premises does your answer rely on?
- Why might someone interpret democracy as a threat?
- If animals had democracy, how might the world be different?
- Is democracy real? How do you know?
- Where is democracy? Can you put your finger on it – literally?
- What is democracy like?
- How might you develop your essay so that it gets to the core of the issue?
- For what reasons might a person find democracy problematic?

- Under what circumstances would you accept a suspension of democracy? Why?

In the 'exemplar questions' section of this book there are many questions which can be used to challenge students' thinking. This includes the subsection covering philosophical questions linked to the various subjects which form the curriculum.

Philosophical questions are challenging because they ask students to look at the concepts and categories underpinning their own thinking as well as that which they are studying. This means pupils have to question the foundations of their own knowledge, beliefs and actions. In some senses, therefore, philosophical questioning involves getting students to think about thinking. That is why it is likely to prove challenging for them.

Probing Questions

Probing questions are good for making pupils' thinking explicit. They can be used by the teacher to elicit information concerning what students understand, know and think, as well as the reasons behind all this. When asking such questions, better results will ensue if the teacher maintains a fairly gentle, exploratory approach. The converse of this – direct, assertive questioning – will probably stymie student responses and discourage pupils from talking freely and at length (and this is the type of talk we want if we are probing, because more information is presented and we are more likely to find things out which we can use to inform our teaching).

Here are some examples of probing questions:

- What do you mean by that?

- What you just said, could you expand on that?
- How might that play out?
- For what reason?
- Could you give me an example of that?
- What other examples might there be?
- What has led you to think that?
- How did you come to think that?
- What else do you think about X?
- How have you come to that conclusion?

You will notice from the examples that probing questions cause students to think more deeply about the matter in hand. This is because they are being asked to develop that which they have already articulated. This means, necessarily, that they will have to go deeper. Should they not do so, this will be because they are not able to do so, because they are deliberately avoiding doing so, or because they have not understood what is being asked of them. Each point has its own remedy.

Provocative Questions

If Marx was right, doesn't that mean that we are all guilty of exploitation?

Why shouldn't the world be unfair?

Wouldn't society be better if pets were put down before they got to a certain age?

The purpose behind provocative questions is to stimulate pupils' thinking. They motivate by engaging the emotions, turning commonly-held positions upside-down, staking claims, presenting the world in a different or unusual light and challenging assumptions or presuppositions. One must be careful with the use of provocative questions – a little time should be set aside in order to think about exactly what they might provoke. You should also give consideration to the sensitivities of your students. The purpose of provocative questions is to stimulate pupil thinking, not to create discord or conflict (though *intellectual discord* is often desirable as the first step to greater understanding).

8. Enquiry Questions

Enquiry-based learning is a powerful approach to pedagogy which stands a high possibility of engaging and motivating students. As a result, it is likely to lead to deep learning – that is, learning in which students actively come to terms with things in their own minds, as opposed to learning in which knowledge is acquired or assimilated as nothing more than a thing in itself. Before we look at enquiry questions, it is worth thinking briefly about this idea of deep learning.

The phrase is somewhat vague. Yet, at the same time, it offers a metaphor which strains towards something we think to be the case. This is especially so if we contrast it with its opposite – shallow or surface learning.

It might be best to think of the word 'deep' in the context of its synonym 'profound' and some of the further terms with which that is associated – multifaceted, multi-layered, meaningful and the phrase 'full of meaning'. Deep learning can be thought of as referring to learning which goes beyond simply being familiar with something, knowing what it is or being able to regurgitate verbatim an item that has been memorised.

The reason why enquiry-based instruction stands a high chance of leading to meaningful, multifaceted learning is because it is purposeful and directed. Therefore, the student has a stake in what is going on and a reason to be involved. If your faculties are engaged, it is much more likely that you will think actively about what is happening. If you are thinking actively, it is inevitable that your experience of your own learning is more likely to be profound (or, even, just closer to profound than might otherwise be the case).

Now we will return to enquiry questions.

We have already noted how questions can be used to frame lessons and activities. We have spent time thinking about discussion and some of the ways in which questions can be used to shape discussion tasks. The points made do not need to be reiterated. As a result, presented here are some brief guidelines on developing enquiry questions, based on what we have already noted elsewhere:

- Enquiry questions should cause students to enquire.
- They should, therefore, be based on a subject. It is into this subject that students will enquire.
- Students are likely to be more motivated by interesting questions.
- If you are not sure what an interesting question looks like, ask your students.
- It should be possible for students to reach some kind of endpoint in their enquiry. This does not necessarily mean finding a final answer.
- Questions should, therefore, be written with some prospective endpoints in mind. The teacher ought to have

an idea of where students might be able to get to with the questions.

- Do not feel obliged to have one question. A whole host of enquiry questions could be derived from a single topic, with students then choosing which one they want to pursue.
- Work with pupils to come up with questions. Present then with some stimulus material and guide them in constructing a series of questions.
- If a question is not working, change it. What sounds great in theory does not always work out in practice.
- If necessary, provide a series of sub-questions which pupils can use to guide their enquiry into the main question.

9. Exam-Style Questions

Practicing exam-style questions is one of the key steps to assessment success. Here are five activities you can use with your students:

1. **This activity is appropriate once pupils have some experience of exam-style questions.** Give every pupil a slip of paper and ask them to write an exam-style question on it. You might what to specify an area of the syllabus to which these questions should refer. When students have written their questions, collect in the slips of paper, shuffle them and then redistribute them. Pupils attempt whatever question they are given. The activity is concluded in one of two ways. Either student answers are taken in, shuffled and redistributed for marking, or answers are returned to the question-authors for marking. The latter approach is

made easier if students write their names on their slips of paper.

2. **Students work in groups of two or three. Each group is given a piece of paper containing five exam-style questions.** Beneath each question there is space in which to write. Groups are invited to work through the various questions and to analyse what a high-level response ought to contain. The teacher indicates a range of areas which should be considered in each case. For example: command words, content and concepts. When sufficient time has elapsed, groups are called on to share their ideas and a discussion ensues. Finally, the teacher asks students to choose one of the questions and to produce a full answer. These are then peer-assessed.

3. **As an extension task**, ask students to write an exam-style question based on what they have being studying in the lesson. As a super-extension task, ask students to answer their question, or to swap questions with a peer and to answer that question instead.

4. **Students work in groups of three or four. Each group is given a large sheet of paper and an exam-style question.** One member of each group writes the group's question at the top of their piece of paper. Groups are given five minutes to discuss the question. They are reminded that they are not trying to answer it as they would do in an exam, rather they are discussing the subject of the question, the different approaches one could take in order to answer it, and the various things which might form part of an answer. One member of each group notes down the

key points on their piece of paper. When the five minutes are up, groups swap pieces of paper and repeat the exercise with a new question. This continues until the teacher decides that discussion has been exhausted. A follow-up could involve all the sheets of paper being placed at the front of the room and students choosing one question to answer in full. They would use the pieces of paper to help them do this.

5. **Students work in groups of three. Each group is given an exam-style question and a large piece of paper.** Groups are asked to create a map of their question. This map should include all the different concepts, ideas, evidence, examples, theories and so on that could be visited during the course of an answer. The various elements should be placed in different parts of the map and supplemented by illustrations. Groups are then invited to walk around the room and to examine the maps their peers have created. A piece of blank paper should be placed beneath each map. As groups look at each other's creations, they should note down on the blank paper anything they think has been missed. They should also provide a rationale as to why it should have been included.

10. Open and Closed Questions

This book as a whole is weighted in favour of open questions. With that said, it does not seek to ignore closed questions. Nor does it seek to deny the efficacy of closed questions at certain times and in certain cases. This section will provide us with an opportunity to look at the structure of open and closed questions as well as a chance to consider their relative merits.

Open Questions

We might think of open questions like this: ‹

The question is the starting point. From this, different possible responses branch out. A variety of different paths can be explored. In a discussion, we might end up a long way from where we started, but we would be able to trace our way back if we wanted to.

Open questions invite many potential answers, all of which may lead to new points and positions. They have the function of providing a multitude of opportunities for response, with these being limited by the content of the question, not its form.

Here are some examples of open questions:

1.1 What do you think?
1.2 Why might this be true?
1.3 What do you like doing?
1.4 How could we solve this?
1.5 Why?

Here is some analysis of the structure of each of these questions:

1.1 This is a question which is wide open. We can infer that it has been said in reference to something and that the question is really: 'What do you think about X?' It invites the respondent to articulate their thinking and places few other demands on them. When this question is asked, it is usually accompanied by a sense that the questioner wants to know the thoughts of the other person and that they are genuinely interested in what it is they think.

1.2 This question is open yet also circumscribed. The words 'be true' delimit the area of possible responses. The questioner has not asked: 'Why might this be true or not?' Of course, a respondent might take this to be the question, but in so doing they would be interpreting. The use of the word 'this' signifies the subject of the question and the words 'Why might' offer us an open command, suggesting that many responses are possible – as long as they refer to the case of the 'this' in question being true.

1.3 This question is open but more heavily circumscribed than the previous one. It is assumed that the respondent does indeed like doing things. It is also implied that these things will equate to common standards of what one might like to do. At the same time, the question is not specifying a specific thing which the respondent is to consider – instead it is the overall category of 'things one likes to do'.

1.4 This question is similar to 1.2. It is open yet circumscribed. The words 'solve this' specify that, while many answers are possible, they must all refer to the attempted solution of the problem which is indicated. The question is included to demonstrate how different formulations may have similar functions and thus make similar demands in terms of response-elicitation.

1.5 This question is open, but not as open as it may at first seem. It invites a broad range of responses yet, at the same time, carries an undertone which signals that any response must be amenable to reason. If one asks the question 'why?' and receives a response such as: 'Because giraffes are pink', one would be entitled to expect an alternative, more appropriate answer.

Drawing all this together, we can note a few common points regarding open questions:

- They invite a range of possible responses.
- They can remain open even while the range of responses is circumscribed.
- They often carry implicit messages about what sort of response is considered appropriate.
- They have a main subject.
- They have a second subject – the respondent's thinking about the main subject.

Closed Questions

We can reverse our symbol and think of closed questions as being like this: ˃

Closed questions narrow down the options, specifying quite strictly what it is that the respondent's answer ought to be about. Here are some examples:

1.1 How old are you?
1.2 Where do you live?
1.3 What time is it?
1.4 Is this true or false?
1.5 What does 'sentiment' mean?

The following points are true for each of these cases:

- The questions specify what type of answer is to be given (number; place; time; true or false; definition).
- The questions demand a response which is likely to be highly specific.
- The questions request information.
- The questions request information which could be verified.
- The questions are definitive. This is expressed through the words 'are', 'do', 'is' and 'does'.

Bearing these five points in mind, we can see that there will be times when closed question are highly appropriate. For example, if we want to check knowledge, ensure accurate recall or find out a specific piece of information.

The risk is that closed questions end up being overused in the classroom. There are two reasons why this might happen.

First, closed questions are quick – both in their saying and in their answering. If one feels pushed for time or if one wants to increase the pace of a lesson, it can be tempting to fall back on closed questions.

Second, they are a simple way to create a sense of progress – although this may often be illusory. When asking closed questions, one can often find someone who is able to say the correct answer. This is no guarantee that they have understood why it is correct though. In fact, it could simply be a guess. In an exchange based on closed questions, very little information is usually elicited:

Teacher: What is 3 divided by 40?

Student: 0.075

Teacher: Fantastic! You're a genius!

But are they? Perhaps their friend told them. Perhaps they used a calculator. Perhaps they guessed. Perhaps they spent the whole night memorising the answer to that question in the hope that it might come up.

Here is a cautionary tale which demonstrates the lack of information elicited by closed questions:

A police officer is in court. He is giving evidence. In his evidence he has claimed that he can identify the two people the prosecution suggests have committed a crime. These two people are the defendants. The barrister asks him if he was wearing his glasses on the night when the crime was committed. He replies that he was not. The barrister asks him how close he came to the people who were committing the crime. He indicates that he came to within twenty feet before they escaped. The barrister inquires as to whether he is short-sighted or long-sighted. The policeman responds that he is short-sighted. The barrister asks him to read out his prescription. The policeman obliges. The barrister asks when the prescription was given. The policeman indicates that it was given three months ago, when he last had his eyes tested. The barrister indicates to the judge that he has no further questions.

A tense atmosphere has descended on the courtroom. The attention of all those present is on the witness. The only noise is the slow clicking of the barrister's heels on the wooden floor as he returns to his seat.

The defence advocate rises to re-examine the witness.

He walks forward, stops and looks up. 'Tell me,' he says, 'do you wear contact lenses when you are at work?'

'Yes I do,' the policeman replies. 'Without fail.'

The final word then, is one of temperance. Closed questions do very specific things. This is their strength but also their weakness. They should not be relied upon to any great extent in the classroom – but nor should they be ignored altogether. A balance is required. One which favours open questions but which does not reject closed ones.

11. Using Questions to Draw out and Develop Reasoning

Reasoning is central to education. It underpins almost the entire curriculum. It is a tool which is absolutely integral to our understanding of the world and of our own selves. If someone cannot reason then much of what we think of as life will remain forever distant to them. Reason helps us to see. Not everything, that is for sure, for faith may be said to begin wear reason ends. Yet, without reason, we have but a little light through which to illumine the darkness.

Again and again, often without any recognition of what we are doing, we urge, cajole and enthuse students to reason:

Why?

What reasons do you have for that?

Why might that be true?

How can you say that?

Can you explain why you think that?

Reasoning comes in various forms. It includes the attribution of cause, the justification of assertion, the deduction from premises, the inferring from evidence and the assessment of likelihood from that which is already known. There is more besides, but this is not the place to explore the nature of reasoning. Instead, here are five methods you might employ so as to draw out and develop reasoning:

1. Appoint two or three 'reason-police'. These students are each given a sheet of card on which a question is written of the type noted above. During discussions, these pupils must listen carefully to what is said. If they hear someone say something and they believe that the reasoning has not been stated or has not been made clear, the students should raise their cards and draw attention to the fact. The speaker is then obliged to answer the questions on the cards.

   This method works with all types of discussion. In whole-class discussion, the 'reason-police' draw attention to themselves whenever they feel it is appropriate. In paired or group discussion, they move around the room, listening in to the conversations which are taking place. As soon as they hear something which requires further reasoning, they hold their cards up and indicate that they have done so to whichever pair or group they are listening to.

2. If you are engaging in a discussion or a debate around a central question, give students an opportunity to develop

their reasoning before the talk begins. Provide each member of the class with a piece of paper. The key question should be written at the top this. Underneath, spaced out so that there is room in which to write, there should be four further questions: What do you think? What is your first reason for thinking this? What is your second reason for thinking this? What is your third reason for thinking this?

Students fill their sheets in before the discussion or debate begins. They can then use these to help them reason more clearly and carefully during the course of the activity.

3. This method is appropriate for whole-class discussions. When a student makes a claim or an assertion (a statement not supported by reasons or evidence), stop the discussion and ask the class: 'What reasons might Student X have for thinking this?' Give some time in which your pupils can consider the question, or ask them to speak about it in pairs. When everyone is ready, ask various students to share their thoughts.

Two things can follow from this point. First, you can turn the discussion towards an analysis and evaluation of the various reasons which have been put forward. Second, you can return to the original speaker and ask how the reasons put forward compare to their own thinking. If they indicate that their original comment was made without the support of any reasons, ask them to decide which of those suggested they feel are most suitable.

4. Socratic questioning. This is explained in more detail in my book, 'How to use Discussion in the Classroom.' I do not want to repeat myself here. Suffice to say, Socratic questioning involves using the four roles taken on by Socrates at various points in Plato's dialogues – those of midwife, ignoramus, gadfly and stingray. The first role sees one helping to deliver ideas through supportive questioning. The second role sees one playing dumb in order to draw out reasoning. The third role sees one continually asking questions so as to compel the speaker to look at all aspects of what they have said. The fourth role involves asking questions which shock the speaker into thinking differently about what they have said.

    Each of these roles can be used by the teacher to help draw out and develop reasoning. One ought to take on the general mind-set of being an educational cross-examiner. The purpose is to improve thinking by making it more rational, reasoned and logical. The method is cross-examination. The tools are the various types of question one can ask.

5. Provide students with a small card which they keep on their desks or in the front of their books. This is their 'reason-card'. The card should contain a selection of questions which students can ask of any piece of writing they have done which ought to include clear reasoning.

    The questions can take one of two forms. On the one hand, they may involve a series of questions concerned with checking: Have you used reasons? Have you explained why you have given the answers you have?

What reasons have you given for your conclusions? On the other hand, they may involve a series of questions concerned with reasoning in general: Why? What reasons are there for that? How might you explain that more clearly? In the latter case, students will ask the questions of each part of their work in turn.

12. Questions from Students

So far, we have been largely concerned with how teachers might use questions in the classroom. It is likely that students will also ask questions. In fact, it is good to encourage them to do so. This is because it fosters a sense of enquiry, encourages them to think independently and leads to them being actively engaged with the learning. Here are five ways in which you might include student questioning in your lessons:

1. Make it clear to pupils that you welcome their questions. Provide a variety of routes by which they might ask you questions. Three such routes are: putting your hand up, writing a question in your book, writing a question on a slip of paper and handing it in to the teacher. By giving a number of routes you will avoid two pitfalls. First, the possibility that a succession of questions will interrupt the flow of an activity or create so many transitions that behaviour takes a downward turn. Second, the possibility that some students will not favour a certain way of asking questions and so will avoid asking them altogether. By providing multiple routes, it is likely that all pupils will find at least one approach which suits them.

2. At the beginning of a unit of work, set up an activity in which the class decides what questions are to frame the lessons which are to come. I would suggest doing this as follows: Divide the class into groups. Assign each group a lesson (lesson 1, lesson 2 and so on). Give each group a set of resources. These should be about the aspect of the topic you want to cover in their lesson. Invite the groups to look through the resources and to then discuss their thoughts. When they have done this, they should pick out what they think is most interesting and use it to create some questions they would like answered. Point out that the questions should be sufficiently 'big' to warrant a whole lesson of investigation. Each group then settles on a single question. This will be used to frame their lesson. The teacher collects the questions in and uses them to inform their planning.

3. Appoint two or three 'question-spotters'. During activities which involve discussion, these students walk around the room listening to the conversations of their peers. They should carry a clipboard or notebook with them and a pen. Every time they hear a good question they write it down and make a note of who said it. At the end of the activity, the 'question-spotters' share with the class some of the best questions they heard. For each question, they explain why it was good and what benefits it brought to the people involved. The class congratulates all the students whose questions were spotted.

If this method is employed regularly, and if praise is consistently given to all students whose questions are spotted, two things are likely to occur. First, pupils will think carefully about the questions they are asking. This is because they will want to ask good questions in the hope of them being spotted and subsequently commended. Second, because the question-spotters will be explaining why the various questions are good, students will get a better understanding of how to structure high-quality questions.

4. Have students lead activities during your lessons in which you would normally do a lot of questioning. For example: a starter activity, a discussion task or a reflective plenary. The student who takes on the role of teacher (or students – a few could do it together) will ask questions in your place. You might want to provide them with some time in advance to prepare; this will depend on who the student is and how confident they are with the task.

5. Plan activities in which students have to use questioning for specific purposes. A number of activities of this type are outlined in chapter four.

13. Questions as a Diagnostic Tool

Questions elicit information. In a number of the previous entries we have looked closely at this in order to consider what questions we might ask and why, exactly, we might ask them. In addition, we have considered how questions can be used as a means to make students' thinking explicit; to bridge the gap between minds; and to give the teacher information through which they can alter and adapt their teaching. This entry draws these various strands together under a common theme: using questions as a diagnostic tool.

To diagnose something is to identify, detect and establish. It involves eliciting information which can be compared to other information independent of the thing in question so that a statement can be made concerning what the questioner believes to be the case. A doctor diagnoses illness. They ask their patients questions in order to get information. They may also examine them and look at their medical history and the history of illness in their family. This information is then brought together and considered in reference to that which the doctor knows. A further source may be called upon – perhaps a textbook or a second opinion. If uncertainty remains, tests might be scheduled, the purpose of these being the obtaining of more information.

Let us think for a moment about a simple case, one in which the doctor does not need further sources or to schedule tests. In this case, they note that the information which they have acquired fits with the knowledge they have concerning a certain type of common disease. The doctor is able to diagnose this common disease by identifying that which the patient displays and conveys as commensurate with that which has been found to signify the disease in question. The doctor is not certain in their diagnosis – they appreciate that there is always room for error – but they are confident that it is correct and that it represents what is most likely to be the case. They prescribe a remedy or a palliative in accordance with what they have diagnosed.

Doctors are concerned with the human body and the human mind. Their area of expertise is medicine. When they question, they do so in order to elicit the information which they feel will be relevant given the circumstances. It is likely that in most cases this information will be of a type that can be referenced to the doctor's knowledge and understanding of medicine.

Teachers are concerned with human thought and human action as it manifests in the developing child. Their area of expertise is not quite as clear cut as that of doctors. The word 'education' is not precise. This is because it is catch-all for disparate aspects rather than a signifier of a discrete discipline. Teachers need to be knowledgeable about a range of things: pedagogy, learning, specific subjects, thinking and psychology (more lay than professional). Unlike the doctor, they do not need to know about any of these in significant depth. It is likely that they will know more about one area than the others, but their skill will come from a synthesis of the various elements.

This presents a small quandary which must be cleared up if a teacher is to use questioning for effective diagnosis. Namely: What is being diagnosed? We can put pedagogy to one side as this concerns what the teacher does or how they set up their lessons. This leaves us with four elements: learning, the specific subject, thinking and psychology.

If a teacher is using questioning in order to diagnose and then prescribe, they should first consider which of these they are most concerned with. This will help them to ask questions which are more appropriate and to look for information which is most relevant. Of course, these factors do not sit independently from one another. They interact and exert varying degrees of influence. As such, the teacher should always be aware of all four, even if they choose to focus on one specifically.

Here is some analysis of the four elements. This can help inform a teacher's decision about what it is they are looking to diagnose:

Learning: This refers to the general act of learning. It includes aspects such as how a student learns, how they interact with what the teacher is asking them to do, what they perceive learning as involving, their general attitude to learning and that which might prevent them from learning. If a student does not appear to be grasping what is going on in class, the teacher may question them in order to try and diagnose why this is the case. They may come to find that the student does not understand what a task ought to entail and how it will help them. The teacher can 'cure' this by explaining and exemplifying for them.

The specific subject: This refers to the content of the lesson. It includes aspects such as knowledge of key terms, understanding of concepts, the ability to complete certain processes, being able to explain how things work and so on. If a student says they do not understand the work, this may be because they cannot come to terms with the content. Diagnostic questioning in this case would help the teacher to identify what specifically the student does not understand. For example, perhaps they have misunderstood a key concept and are now running into difficulties because they are wrongly contextualising new material they encounter. The teacher could follow up their questioning by rectifying the student's earlier error. They could then demonstrate how this change makes it easier to understand the new material.

Thinking: This refers to the general notion of thinking. It includes aspects such as reasoning, analysis, making connections, problem-solving and so on. A student might give you an answer to a question that does not include any evidence of how or why they have come to that answer. Diagnostic questioning can then be used in order to draw out the thinking which led the student to give their answer. It may be that the student's thinking was sound. If this was the case, it will still have been better to make the process explicit.

On the other hand, it may be that the student came to the correct answer through incorrect means. In this case, the questioning will have exposed the error, giving the teacher an opportunity to correct it (most likely involving an exploration of the thinking in conjunction with the student).

Psychology: This refers to the psychological factors which are at play in the classroom. It includes aspects such as motivation, self-confidence, the influence of past experience, self-esteem and so on. If a student is reluctant to engage with a particular task, it may be due to a psychological factor which is creating inhibitions. Diagnostic questioning can be used to try and find out what precisely is the issue. The teacher can use the information they gain to suggest alternative approaches. For example, a pupil might be reluctant to take part in group work intended to lead to a presentation. Diagnostic questioning might reveal that they are scared of speaking in front of a large audience. The teacher could then use this information to suggest that they have a scripting role in the group and do not have to speak, that they produce a written piece of work instead, or that groups present to each other rather than to the whole class.

In summary:

- Diagnostic questioning involves asking questions in order to elicit information for a specific purpose.
- This purpose will most likely be problem-solving, the identification of error or the checking of what is known or understood.

- The specific area of focus will influence what questions are asked and how they are asked.

A final note regarding the whole class

Diagnostic questioning concerned with thinking can be used with all the students in a class at the same time. Here is how to do it:

1. Provide a means whereby all students can make their thinking known to you. The simplest method is using mini-whiteboards.
2. Plan a series of questions based on the most common misconceptions concerning the topic.
3. Display or ask these questions in turn.
4. Ask students to respond using the method on which you have settled (for example, mini-whiteboards).
5. Use discussion to explore the answers which are given. Identify and talk about any misconceptions. Rectify these errors, or let other students rectify them, and discuss why they occurred in the first place and how they can be avoided in future.

14. Serial Questioning

Questions often come in a series during the course of a lesson. Examples of this include when the teacher is questioning students one-on-one, when they are leading a discussion or when they set some written work. Developing such series in advance has a distinct advantage. It gives the teacher time and space in which to consider how best to move students' learning forward from a particular starting point. Here are three examples demonstrating this:

Planning a series of questions for use in a one-on-one setting

Let us imagine that you have a particularly able student in one of your classes. This student completes work quickly and correctly and always gets onto the extension tasks. You decide that, while other students are finishing the main task, you would like to question them one-on-one in order to challenge and stretch their thinking. You have noticed that, although the student is very able, they do not necessarily go beyond the information given and think 'outside of the box'. Your questioning will focus on encouraging them to do this.

The topic is the Industrial Revolution. Students have been set the task of analysing three sources – one from a child labourer, one from a factory owner and one from a member of parliament. You might plan the following series of questions to use with the student who is particularly able:

How might we argue that the three sources are biased?

What do we mean by the word 'bias?'

Is it possible for any source to be without bias? Why?

With these three sources here, would it be possible to eliminate bias?

Have you been biased when writing about the sources? How do you know?

Would it be a problem if you were biased? Why?

Why might a historian be criticised for being biased?

If a historian wrote without any bias, would it not just be a succession of facts?

You will note that the concept of bias has been fixed on and that the teacher is encouraging the student to interrogate this (and, in the process, their own understanding). The questions follow a clear line of development. They move from a starting point connected to the three sources, to a much more abstract and speculative position. This results in the level of challenge gradually rising through the course of the questioning.

Planning a series of questions for use in a discussion

Let us imagine that you are starting a new topic with a class. You decide to show them a short film clip which contains information about various elements of the topic in question. This will act as a stimulus from which a discussion will develop. You plan to start students off in pairs and to then build up a whole-class discussion.

The topic is human rights and the questioning might be as follows:

Questions to discuss in pairs:

Why might the film have been made?

What did you think about the film?

Which bits of the film did you think were most interesting and why?

Questions to discuss as a whole class:

What do we already know about human rights?

What might the film clip have to do with human rights?

If you were making a film about human rights, what might you include in it?

What questions do you have about human rights?

How might we try and answer these questions during the unit of work?

You will note that the questions for the pairs are designed to draw out student responses whereas the questions for the whole class are intended to build up a picture of students' knowledge concerning human rights. By planning two such series in advance, one is able to consider how the first can connect to the second – the paired discussion is thus made into a platform for the group discussion, with the two together forming a starting point for the unit of work as a whole.

Planning a series of questions for use in written work

Let us imagine that you are setting students an assessment. This is to be based on their previous six weeks of study, during which they have learnt about pacifism and religion. The assessment might consist of a series of questions such as the following:

1. What does pacifism mean?
2. Can you give two examples of pacifism?
3. Why might people decide to be pacifists?
4. What religious beliefs might lead people to become pacifists?
5. Can you give two examples of how pacifism has led to changes in the world?

6. Why might religious believers disagree about whether you should be a pacifist or not?

7. Why might someone argue that pacifism brings you closer to God?

8. Do you agree with the arguments from the previous question? Why?

9. Why might some religious believers argue that pacifism is a bad thing?

10. 'Everyone who is religious should be a pacifist.' Do you agree or disagree? Why might someone think differently to you?

You will note that the difficulty level of the questions increases. The later ones are more demanding and require students to manipulate concepts, make accurate use of their knowledge and develop reasoned arguments – with which they may or may not agree. In addition, the later questions are more discursive, giving students the opportunity to develop their thinking in depth and to demonstrate their understanding of the topic.

The key point made by the example is that a series of written questions can be underpinned by a larger purpose, the like of which could not be ascribed to any one of the questions individually. Considering in advance what that purpose is makes the planning of such a series simpler. It also leads to greater coherency – which is of benefit to teachers and students alike.

15. Choosing the Subject Matter of Questions

This list contains some of the things which questions you use in the classroom might be about:

- Concepts
- Events
- Processes
- Interpretations
- Pieces of information
- Ways of thinking
- Opinions
- Arguments
- Ideas
- Speculations
- Possibilities
- Alternatives
- Assumptions
- Theories
- Experiments
- Facts
- Words
- Actions
- Beliefs
- Knowledge
- Understanding
- Feelings
- Reasons
- Examples
- Evidence

It is well worth observing and analysing your own questioning in order to assess what you are asking students about. This will help you to be more aware of the type of questions you are using and the particular subjects to which you return. I know that, when it comes to my own teaching, I tend to ask more questions to do with ideas and understanding than to do with facts and knowledge. I find it helpful to be aware of this as it encourages me to give attention to the opposite side of things from time to time.

It is not worth trying to reach a perfect balance of questions – no such thing exists. Better instead to play to your own strengths while being aware of those areas you may neglect (you can then make sure you give them attention from time to time).

Chapter Four – Activities

In this chapter we explain and exemplify twenty different activities based around questioning. All of these are generic and can be used across the curriculum and with a variety of age-groups. In some cases, minor adjustments will need to be made to take account of the particular class you are teaching.

1. Cross-Examination

Students are divided into groups of four. One member of each group is designated as a cross-examiner. The cross-examiners leave their groups and stand at the front of the class. The teacher hands each of the groups a pack of information about a different area of the topic. Examples could include: different sources related to an event; different perspectives on an issue; different poems and interpretations from a certain genre.

The cross-examiners split up and go to each group in turn, asking questions in order to elicit information about the material which has been handed out. They should make notes as they go. When they have visited all the groups, they return to their original group and share what they have learnt. Students then consider the information they have gained and assess what conclusions they can draw from it.

An overarching question can be used to frame the activity. Students are expected to try to answer this through their cross-examinations and through their subsequent evaluations of the material. Alternatively, you might like to use the activity at the start of a topic as a way of introducing pupils to the new area of study. In such cases, you could provide a generic question such as:

'What might we look at in our next sequence of lessons?' to frame the activity.

It is likely that there will be a short period of downtime when the cross-examiners are stood at the front of the class and the groups are analysing the material you have distributed. To keep the cross-examiners focussed, ask them to discuss as a group the sort of questions they might ask. Encourage them to consider how different types of questions will elicit different types of responses. In addition, you might ask them to identify a clear purpose which is to direct their questioning (and to provide a justification for this).

Develop the activity by giving each group written instructions to inform their interactions with the cross-examiner. For example, one group might be instructed to only give away certain information if questions of a specific type are asked. This will help to encourage the cross-examiners to think carefully about the questions they are asking.

2. Roving Reporters

Divide the class into two groups. One group are 'roving reporters' and the other group are role-players. Provide the latter group with character cards detailing what roles they are to play. It will help if they are given background information to contextualise their character's behaviour, thoughts and interactions. The roving reporters are given a pro-forma containing a table. The names of each of the different characters are written in this. There is space beside or beneath each of the names. It is in this space that the reporters will write down what they find out.

The activity begins and the reporters mingle with the role-players. It may be that you have sufficient character cards so that each role-player is a different person. If not, you will have to repeat characters. It will not matter if certain characters are played by a number of students. The key is to make sure there are a range of characters and that each student has a role.

The reporters' job is to speak to each of the characters indicated on their sheet and to elicit as much information from them as possible. You might like to put a limit on the number of questions they are allowed to ask each person to whom they talk. This will really focus the reporters' minds and push them to think carefully about what questions they are asking and why.

At the end of the activity, each reporter should pair up with a role-player. It is their job to then share what they have found out. In turn, the role-player can assess whether the information discovered about their character is accurate or not. Finally, the pairs can work together to create a news report or article detailing all the information which has been elicited (facts could be checked with the various role-players if necessary).

A great way to use this activity is if you have an event, idea, theory or some other such item about which a number of people or groups hold different views. An example would be a case study looking at the placement of a wind farm. The various groups concerned with this would include environmentalists, conservationists, local residents, local businesses, the energy company, national government, local government and so on. Clearly there is a good range here, enough so that many students will be able to take on different characters. In addition, there will be lots for the reporters to find out. The task could culminate with a report being written for an independent tribunal about whether or not the wind farm should be placed in the local area.

3. Detective Inspectors

Divide the class into groups of three. Give each group a number (you might want to make this really clear by printing large numbers on sheets of paper and handing these out). Give each group a set of resources which deal with a part of the overall topic (if you have a large number of groups, you may end up giving a couple of groups the same material). Explain that each group's job is to find out what the big picture is and how the information they have been given fits into this. Students will be acting as detectives who are trying to uncover all the parts of the story.

Groups begin by familiarising themselves with their resources. They then find another group with whom to pair up. The activity is more dramatic if groups sit facing each other, with a table in between them as a barrier.

There are three rules which students need to be aware of at this stage:

1. Groups must take it in turns to ask one question at a time.
2. They are only allowed to ask five questions of the other group.
3. Groups are not allowed to show each other their resources – they are only allowed to answer the questions that are asked.

Students should be provided with a pro-forma containing the same number of boxes as there are groups. They write the group numbers at the top of each box and make a note of the answers they receive underneath.

The activity continues until all possible pairings have been made. At this point, students return to their original positions and discuss their findings. The teacher should provide some questions to structure this, for example: What is the big picture? How does our information connect to what other people know? What do we still need to find out? You might like to give groups the opportunity to ask three more questions of any of the other groups. This will allow them to address gaps in their knowledge.

The activity concludes with a discussion. This will involve the various groups putting forward their theories about the big picture and how their information connects; explanation from some of the groups of what their material focussed on; and an evaluation of the questioning which took place and the results to which it gave rise.

4. Questions, Soft To Tough

This activity is good to use at the end of a unit of study. Here is how it works:

Divide the class in half. The two groups will, eventually, be facing off against one another. Before this, each half should split into pairs or threes (depending on the number of students). We will refer to these as the sub-groups.

The sub-groups are instructed to develop a series of ten questions based on the topic they have been studying. The questions must start out easy and get progressively harder. The tenth question should be the toughest of them all. There is, however, one caveat. Students must be able to answer their own questions. If they cannot do this, they are not allowed to ask the question.

When sufficient time has elapsed, pupils are asked to rearrange the room so that there is a long row of tables with chairs placed either side (or two rows if you have a lot of students). The two halves of the class then sit themselves on either side of the row. The teacher labels one half as 'A' and one half as 'B'.

Group 'A' are invited to go first. Each pupil should ask their ten questions to the student sat opposite. That student tries to answer the questions. The two pupils then discuss the answers, with the questioner correcting any mistakes. The groups then swap over, with the 'B' students asking their questions to the 'A' students.

When this is done, Group 'A' are invited to stand up and to change seats. The process is repeated with the new pairings. It will be best if students do not move to the seat next to where they are sat. This is because the student who is sat opposite may have heard their questions (and answers) during the first phase of the activity. The activity concludes with a whole-class discussion in which students analyse and evaluate the questions which caused the greatest difficulties. In addition, this provides an opportunity for the students who developed those questions to speak about how and why they created them.

5. The Big Pitch

Divide students into groups of four. One of these groups is designated the 'executive board'. The rest of the groups, the pitchers, are set a problem for which they must develop a solution. The groups then work as follows:

Executive Board: They are given background information on the problem which they must read and analyse. They then discuss the problem and talk about what possible solutions they think their peers might put forward. Next, the group work together to come up with a set of criteria they will use to judge the pitches they receive. Finally, the group develop a range of questions they will ask to the pitchers.

Pitchers: Each group works together to create a solution to the problem. The teacher displays a range of things which must be done. This will include: create a solution to the problem; prepare a short presentation explaining your solution; plan a speech in which you extol the virtues of your solution; and anticipate what questions you might be asked about your solution and how you will respond to these.

Two further things may happen during the problem-solving phase. First, you may invite one member from each group to visit the executive board in order to find out what they are looking for from the solutions. Second, you may invite the executive board to walk around the room so that they can observe what the groups are doing and ask them questions if appropriate.

When sufficient time has elapsed, call the solution-development proceedings to a halt. At this point, you should ask the executive board to arrange themselves at the front of the room so that they are sat behind two tables. The tables should be at a forty-five degree angle to the rest of the class. This will ensure the executive board can be seen and heard, but that they can also talk directly to the group who is presenting.

Each group comes up in turn. They pitch their solution to the board in a specified period of time (say two minutes) and then face questions from the executives. After this, members of the class are invited to ask questions as well.

When each group has delivered their pitch, the executive board are invited to retire to the corner of the room (or the corridor) in order to evaluate the pitches and to decide which was best and why. Meanwhile, the teacher asks the groups to reflect on what went well in their presentations and what could have been improved.

The activity concludes with the executive board returning to give their decision. It is important that they support this with reasons and a detailed explanation which references what was said during the course of the pitches.

6. Philosophical Questioning

In the 'exemplar questions' section of this book I have provided a selection of philosophically-informed questions covering various subjects on the curriculum. These can be used to stimulate discussion and as the foundation for enquiry-based tasks in which students work in groups, or independently, to further their understanding of a topic.

Philosophy can be thought of as 'thinking about thinking'. In the context of the classroom, it provides students with an opportunity to analyse the concepts and categories on which their thinking depends, to enquire as to the nature of knowledge and to think about moral issues, amongst other things. Five major branches of philosophy can be relied upon as bases for the formation of questions relevant to most subjects. They are:

- Ethics (the study of morality – What is right and wrong? How can we know?)
- Epistemology (the study of the nature of knowledge – What can we know for certain? How can we come to know things?)
- Metaphysics (the study of the fundamental nature of the world – What is there? What is it like?)
- Aesthetics (the study of the nature of beauty and art – What is art? What causes something to be beautiful?)
- Political Philosophy (the study of politics, authority, justice and so on – Why should I be governed? What is just?)

If, as a teacher, you familiarise yourself with these branches, it will be easy for you to spot opportunities during lessons when an activity might be turned in a philosophical direction.

Three major benefits stem from taking advantage of such opportunities:

- You will cause students to think more deeply about the subject and topic. This will help to develop their understanding.
- You will help students to clarify their thinking.

- You will cause students to think critically about the concepts and categories they use, as well as the ideas and arguments they put forward.

For me, personally, philosophical thinking is an end in itself. You may not feel the same and, should this be the case, these concrete benefits can provide a reason as to why you might promote philosophical thinking during the course of your teaching.

7. Who Am I?

This is a very simple game which is also a lot of fun. It works as follows:

The class is divided into groups of two or three. Each student is given a Post-It® note. They write the name of a specific person (for example, Queen Elizabeth) or a representative of a group (for example, a member of the working class) on this, making sure to keep it secret.

One member of each group elects to go first. They are passed a Post-It® note by one of their peers, making sure not to look as they receive it. They stick this on their forehead. They now have to work out who they are by asking questions to the other members of their group. When the student correctly works out who they are – or when they give up – the next student takes their turn.

You might develop the activity in any of the following ways:

1. Students are only allowed to ask questions which can be answered 'yes' or 'no'.
2. Students are only allowed to ask a certain number of questions.
3. Students are only allowed to ask written questions (responses must be written as well).
4. If students are working in a group of three, the two pupils who answer the questions decide in advance which one of them will tell the truth and which one of them will tell lies. The student who is asking the questions must try to work out what information they receive is true and what is false.
5. Students are not allowed to ask direct questions. Instead, they must ask indirect question such as: 'Who is this person like?' 'How might this person react in situation X?' 'How might this person describe person X?'

8. Twenty Questions

This is another simple game with which I am sure you will be familiar. It works as follows:

Either in groups or as a whole class, one person is asked to think of something connected to the topic. You might like to specify a range of categories from which students can select something. The group or the whole class then has twenty questions which they can use to try and discover what the thing in question is. Questions should be phrased such that they can only be answered 'yes' or 'no'.

Here are some ways in which you might develop the game:

1. Appoint a student whose job it is to record the questions that are asked. These can then be discussed at the end of the activity.

2. Appoint a student to record the answers that are given. This will help pupils to keep track of what information has been elicited.

3. Encourage students to choose more abstract or esoteric elements of the topic for others to guess. This will increase the difficulty level of the activity.

4. Precede the activity with a discussion about what makes a good question in this particular game. Draw students' attention to the fact that there is a higher chance of success if one can narrow down the options as early as possible. Talk about what types of questions are likely to have this effect. Finally, you might like to consider with your class when and where such questions might come in useful (beyond the confines of Twenty Questions).

5. Make the game competitive. Divide the class in half and write out a series of slips of paper containing things which connect to the topic. Call a student up from one side and give them a slip of paper at random. Their teammates must try to work out what the thing is in as few questions as possible. The opposing team then have their turn. The game continues for as long as the teacher wishes. A question count is made as the game goes along. The team who asked the fewest questions is the winning team (add on a penalty of twenty questions if a team fails to correctly work out what their word is).

9. If This Is The Answer, What Might Be the Question

This activity is good to use at the start of lessons. It is engaging, pacey and affords students a high chance of success (thus motivating and engaging them). It works as follows:

Display an answer on the board and pose the question: 'If this is the answer, what might be the question?' Invite students to list as many possible questions as they can inside a short space of time (two minutes should suffice). The activity works equally well when students are in pairs as when they work individually. Here are some examples:

Answer: Human Rights

Possible questions: What does everybody have? What stops people being tortured? How can we protect people from governments and dictators?

Answer: Oxbow lake

Possible questions: What do you call a crescent shaped lake? What can erosion create in a meandering river? Of what is the Reelfoot Lake in Tennessee an example?

You might want to caveat the task with a further statement of some kind, for example:

- Come up with as many questions as you can.
- Try to come up with the most unusual question in the class.
- Aim for three questions which are all completely different.
- When you have come up with three questions, consider what other answers you might be able to give to these.

-   Use the word 'justify' in one of your questions.

When students have come up with their questions, choose a few people to share their thoughts with the class. This opportunity can be used to discuss the structure of the questions and to consider why they might be good or how they might be developed.

10. Random Questions

Create a large set of questions which are generic and which can be applied to different material. You could use some of the questions from the 'exemplar questions' section of this book. Write each question on a separate piece of paper and put all the pieces of paper in a box. Keep this in your room – you will be able to use it again and again.

Divide the class into groups of three. Take the box round and present it to each group in turn. Students withdraw a piece of paper and then read out the question. That question is to form the basis of the group's work; they will spend the next part of the lesson discussing and investigating it.

Give students an appropriate amount of time in which to develop some answers to their question. How long you give them will depend to on the topic to which the questions are being applied and the nature of the questions themselves. In some cases, questions are likely to be fairly straightforward and so will require a short period of time to answer. In other cases, questions are likely to be complex or challenging and will therefore require an extended period of time to answer.

When the time is up, invite one member of each group to act as an envoy. They should visit each of the other groups in turn and explain what their question was and what answers they and their colleagues came up with. The activity can end at this point, or, you might like to introduce an additional element wherein the whole class discuss two or three of the questions (you can pick out those which are of most interest or which are likely to generate the most rewarding discussion).

The activity is best used when students have already spent some time studying the topic. This is because they will have greater means at their disposal, with which to engage with the questions. If the activity is done near the start of a unit of work, one risks the chance of students not being able to access the questions; there is a higher possibility of this because the questions are selected at random, rather than being mediated by the teacher.

11. Question Set

Work with your class to develop a set of questions which can be used again and again when doing a specific type of task. Students can then use these each time such a task arises. This will help them to develop their skills in that area and to think methodically. Here are some examples of activities with which a question set could be used:

- Analysing sources
- Interpreting texts
- Developing arguments
- Assessing evidence
- Evaluating theories

Here is an example of a question set based on the first item in the list, analysing sources:

- Who created the source?
- For what reasons might the source have been created?
- How does it compare to other sources?
- Who might have interacted with the source and for what reasons?
- Where might the source have been found?
- Could the source be biased? Why?

As you will note, such a set provides students with a clear focus each time they engage with a source. One of the benefits of using this method is that it trains pupils to approach material in a systematic way. As a result, there is a high likelihood that they will develop the skills required by the activity in a relatively short space of time (due to the uniform repetition).

12. Question Porters

Students are divided into groups of four. One member of each group is designated a 'question porter'. They come to the front of the class where they are given a question by the teacher (you might like to attach this to a stick so that it can be held up in the air). The porters return to their groups and share the question with their peers. Discussion ensues. During this, the porter should make some notes on what is said.

After sufficient time has passed, the teacher asks the porters to stand up and to take their questions to another group. Upon sitting down, the porters share some of the key points which came out of the first discussions. If they wish, they can direct their new group to explore a particular area of the question, a supplemental question or a specific point that came up in the first discussion. This does not have to happen – the new group could simply discuss the question freely – but it is a good option to be able to use with question porters who feel suitably confident.

The whole process is repeated as many times as the teacher feels worthwhile. It is likely that fatigue will set in after three or four rotations. The teacher should be alive to this and be ready to send the question porters back to their original groups when the time is right.

Upon returning to their original groups, the question porters should share with their peers what other groups have said during their discussions. A further discussion could then ensue either lead by the question porter, or predicated on some of the different points which have arisen from the original group's various other discussions (to which the question porter will not have been privy).

This activity can be used at various points, with the questions being adapted accordingly. For example:

1. Use the activity at the end of a unit of work. The various questions are akin to those that might come up in an exam based on the topic.
2. The activity could contain questions which are concerned with concepts central to the topic. If so, it would be well used mid-way through a unit of work. This is because students will be coming to terms with the key concepts but will probably not yet have thought about them in great depth.

3. Use the activity at the beginning of a unit of work. The questions could be concerned with speculation, students' existing knowledge and their prior experience.

13. Interviewing

Here are three ways in which you might use interviewing as the basis of a classroom activity:

1. Explain to students that they will be interviewing their peers in order to ascertain their views, opinions and ideas concerning the area of study. This activity works best at the start of a unit of work or towards the end. In the first case, it acts as a primer, eliciting students' existing knowledge and experience of the topic. It also helps them to start thinking about it academically – something they may not have done before. In the second case, it helps students to reflect on that which they have studied and to draw together all the learning they have done.

Students are given ten minutes in which to come up with five to ten questions (the specific number will depend on how much time you want to give over to the activity) connected to the topic, which they can ask their peers. You can scaffold this by providing a couple of questions of your own to get students started, or by asking more able students to read out some of their questions.

When all members of the class have created their questions, invite them to move around the room and to interview as many of their peers as they can. They should make a note of the responses they receive.

The activity can be concluded in one of two ways. First, you might ask students to write up their findings. Second, you might ask students to discuss their findings in groups of three (this will centre on them comparing and contrasting what their questions have elicited).

2. Students work in pairs. One member of each group is given a character card. They are to role-play this character. As such, the activity will work better if it is done mid-way through a unit of work. This will mean that students have sufficient knowledge and understanding to contextualise the role they are to play.

The other member of each pair is the interviewer. Their job is to ask questions of the role-player and to note down their responses. If there is time, a second set of character cards can be handed out and the members of each pair can swap roles.

The activity can be further developed by having pairs team up and compare the various responses which were elicited during their interviews. This can then lead onto a discussion of the attitudes, beliefs, values and so on of the character (or characters) who were being role-played.

3. The class is introduced to the area of study. A range of categories connected to this are displayed on the board. The teacher divides the class so that the number of groups is equal to the number of categories. Each group is

assigned a category. They have ten minutes to come up with a selection of questions they would like to ask, all of which must be connected to the category in question.

When the time is up, the teacher asks the groups to order their questions from most to least important and to elect a representative whose job it will be to ask the questions. The representatives then come up to the front of the class in turn. Each has three minutes in which to ask the teacher as many questions as they can from their list. The teacher must try to answer the questions as fully and as accurately as possible (and admit if they do not know the answer).

Before the questioning begins, hand out a pro-forma. This should contain a series of boxes, each of which will be labelled with one of the categories. Students can use this sheet to make notes.

14. Focus Groups

Here are two ways to use focus groups as a basis for learning:

1. Randomly select ten students from the class. Arrange a series of desks so that they are pushed together with chairs around them. The chosen pupils sit here, with the teacher at the head of the arrangement. This is the focus group. The rest of the class should seat themselves around the outside.

   The teacher explains that members of the focus group will be invited to share their ideas and opinions on a range of questions relevant to the topic. The students sat around the outside are each given a pro-forma. This contains the questions the teacher will ask, along with space in which to write.

The teacher proceeds by asking the first question. Members of the focus group respond and a discussion develops. Students sat around the outside note down what they think are the most important or the most interesting points arising from the debate.

At the end of the focus group, when all the questions have been asked, those students who were sat in the middle stand up and join their peers who were sat on the outside making notes. Groups of two or three are formed. Each should contain one focus group member and one or two note-taking pupils. Discussion then ensues concerning what was observed. Pupils should also reflect on the points raised during the debate.

One way you might like to alter to this activity is by having students come up with the questions for the focus group. This can be done by placing pupils into groups of three or four and asking each one to put forward a question they believe will prove good for discussion.

2. Divide the class in three (unless you have a small class, in which case either divide it in half or keep it as one). Ask students to arrange the tables and chairs such that there are three collections of desks around which each third of the class can sit.

Ask each group to work together to produce a set of questions connected to the area of study and which could be used as the basis of a focus group discussion. When students have done this, ask them to appoint two members of their group as focus group leaders. These students stand up, take their list of questions with them and move to a different group. Discussion then ensues, based on the lists of questions.

When sufficient time has elapsed, call proceedings to a halt. The focus group leaders should return to their original groups and share the results of the discussion which they chaired. In turn, their peers will share the results of the discussion of which they were a part.

The activity may be concluded here, or it may be suffixed by a whole-class reflection in which a comparison is made between the various discussions which developed as a result of the different question sets which were used.

15. Questioning the Question

When students answer a question or complete a task, it is always of benefit if they first question that which is being asked or requested of them. This causes students to think critically about the matter in hand and to produce a response which is more closely connected to what is at issue than might otherwise be the case. Here are five activities you can use to help students question the question:

1. **Question set.** Provide pupils with a collection of questions which they could ask of any question or task. For example;

- What am I being asked to do?
- What are the key words in the question or task?
- What do these mean?
- Why am I being asked this?
- How will I know that I have achieved what is being asked of me?

These could be displayed for pupils on the board, printed off and handed out to students, or printed out and stuck in the front of their books.

2. **Question set with groups.** As above, except the class is divided into groups and each group given one of the questions from the list. The responses which groups come up with are then shared with the whole class. If appropriate, these could be collated on the board so that students can refer to them while they complete their work.

3. **Question debate.** Four or five assessment-style questions are written on large sheets of paper. These are distributed throughout the room. Pupils are invited to walk around and to write an explanation on each sheet of paper of how they would go about answering the particular question. They should also read what their peers have written. At the end of the activity, pupils select one of the questions and produce a detailed answer. They should use the comments written on the relevant sheet to help them do this.

4. **Question paths.** Display a question on the board. Ask pupils to work in groups of three. Each group creates five pathways representing alternative ways the question could be answered. Each pathway should concentrate on a different aspect of the question, or on a different interpretation of the question.

   When students have finished their pathways, they should discuss the different options and decide which one they will follow through. They then use this as the basis of a written answer.

5. **What will a good answer look like?** This activity is very simple. Display a question for students and then ask them: 'What will a good answer look like?' Collate responses from the whole class (ensuring you also elicit explanations and reasons) and use these as success criteria to guide your pupils in their work.

16. Who, What, Where, When, Why, How?

These six words are the starting point for the majority of questions. They can also be the starting point for a variety of question-based activities. Here are three examples you might like to use in your classroom:

1. Divide the class into six groups. Provide each group with a collection of resources concerning the area of study. Assign one of the question words to each of the groups. Indicate that they should come up with a range of

questions based on that word, and that they should then ask those questions of the material which you have handed out.

At the start of the activity, give students a pro-forma containing six large boxes. These will be labelled with the words 'who, what, where, when, why and how'. In the box which contains the word assigned to their group, pupils will write down the answers they come up with in response to the questions they developed.

When sufficient time has passed, ask groups to elect a representative. These students visit the other groups and share the findings which relate to their particular word. Eventually, each member of the class will have a completed pro-forma and, in turn, a wealth of information about the topic.

2. Take six large sheets of paper. At the top of each sheet, write one of the key words: 'who, what, where, when, why and how'. Distribute these throughout the room. Invite students to walk around and to add questions to each of the pieces of paper (these will be based on the particular word in question). When sufficient time has elapsed, draw the activity to a close.

The sheets of paper can now be stuck up on your classroom wall. Explain to students that they can use these to help them when they are analysing material, taking part in discussions, completing tasks or answering questions. In addition, make it clear that students are free to add to the question sheets whenever they think of new questions.

- Create laminated slips of paper for each class member. These should contain the six question words in the following form: Who...? What...? Where...? When...? Why...? How...?

Encourage students to use these when they are completing tasks, answering questions or taking part in discussions. In effect, the slips will act as an aide memoire for the pupils, helping them to focus their thinking and to engage analytically with the work that has been set. It is also a useful tool for the teacher, who can say: 'Have a look at your question slip' or 'How might you use your question slip?' if a student asks for help (this, in turn, will encourage them to be more independent).

17. Question Stations

Create six or seven different stations around your room (this is working on the premise that you have around thirty students). Each station should be focussed on a different question, all of which should relate to the overall topic of study. This is made clearer if exemplified:

Topic of study:

Democracy in the United Kingdom

Questions:

1. What happens in the Houses of Parliament?
2. Is democracy a perfect system?

3. What features must something have to be called a democracy?
4. How might what we call democracy actually be a pleasant illusion?
5. What is the best way to get involved in politics and why?
6. What might you do to try and change something in your local community?
7. Why might people want democracy in their country?

You will note from the example that some questions (such as number 1) are fairly concrete, whereas other questions (such as number 4) are quite abstract. One of the advantages of this activity is that you can provide your class with a range of question types. This will help you to differentiate, help them to access the work, and help both you and them to think broadly about the topic in question.

Students are given a pro-forma containing the questions which are to be found at each activity station. There is space for them to write. They make notes as they visit each station.

In addition to questions, the stations will contain a variety of other things. Using the example from above, station number one would contain information concerning the House of Commons and the House of Lords. Students would be expected to read, comprehend and analyse this material in order to answer the question. Station number six might have a large sheet of paper with different categories written on it (such as 'to do with crime'; 'to do with young people'; and 'to do with the environment'). Students could then write on this sheet, answering the question in relation to the different categories. This would also allow other students to acquaint themselves with the thoughts of their peers.

At the end of the activity, the teacher asks students to vote for which question they would most like to discuss. A discussion ensues, built on the knowledge that pupils have developed through the course of the activity. If there is time, the second most popular question can be discussed as well.

18. Question Cards

This activity requires some advanced planning. The time that you put in will be well spent though, because you will be able to use the same resources again and again with different content. Here is how it works:

Take a few pieces of card and cut the material up into playing-card-sized segments. The number of segments you create will depend on how many questions you want in your 'deck'. On each card you should write a question which could be asked of a wide variety of different content. Here are some examples:

- What is it?
- How might you describe it?
- What might it connect to?
- Does it have a purpose? What might this be?
- What do you already know about it?
- Where have you come across it before?
- How might it be used/work/function?
- Does it have a structure? If so, what is its structure?
- Why might we be learning about it?
- What do you think we should try and find out about it?

Whatever questions you come up with, they should be generic. It may be that you produce ones which are specific to your subject. You could also use ones from the 'exemplar questions' section of this book. Whichever approach you take, you will end up with a deck of cards containing a range of questions which can be asked of a wide variety of content.

There are a number of ways in which you can use the cards:

1. Put students into groups of three. Give each group a different resource. Draw questions from the deck at random. Ask groups to note down the answers to the questions, in relation to their particular resource, as you go along. Groups can then share their findings at the end of the activity.

2. Give all students the same resource. Draw questions from the deck at random. Ask students to note down their answers individually. Follow this up with a whole-class discussion. This will involve pupils sharing their answers and a general assessment being made of the nature of the resource in question.

3. Create a number of decks. This can be easily achieved by printing off the questions, sticking them onto card and then cutting them out. Put students into groups of three. Give each group is given a resource (this could be the same for all, or different) and a deck of cards. One member of each group is designated as the 'card- person'. They pull cards out at random and ask the questions to the rest of their group. Answers are collated as the activity progresses.

19. Different Questions, Same Material

Divide the class into groups of three. Each group is given the same resources but a different question. Groups try to answer their question by analysing and investigating the resources they have been given. When they have done as much as they feel is possible, they create a presentation of their findings. Next, groups pair up and take it in turns to present to one another. Pairings then split, new pairings are formed and the task is repeated. This continues until groups have presented their findings three or four times (and thus received information about the findings of three or four other groups).

Here is an example:

The topic is crime and deviance. The material given to each group is as follows: a newspaper article about a recent high-profile crime; statistics from the Home Office concerning crime in the United Kingdom; a case study looking at how crime was reduced in a local neighbourhood; three examples of behaviour in other cultures which would be seen as norm-breaking if it was to take place in the United Kingdom; a summary of a sociological study concerning the relative rates of deviance demonstrated by teenage girls and boys.

The following questions could be given to the various groups:

- What does the material tell us about crime in the United Kingdom?
- How might the material help us to understand how deviance is defined?
- How closely linked are crime and deviance?
- Who decides what is deviant?

- Is crime the same in all societies?
- Is crime or deviance a bigger issue in our society? Why?

In this case it would be expected that students had some prior knowledge of the topic. In addition, the teacher might provide textbooks to supplement the material which has been handed out. You will see though, that the structure of the activity is such that it generates a wide range of knowledge from a single starting point.

To develop the activity, you might like to discuss with students how their questions influenced their interactions with the material. It might also be fruitful to explore how the questions led pupils to interpret the material in certain ways, to focus on specific areas, or to ignore certain aspects.

20. Question Assessment

Self-assessment and peer-assessment are integral parts of good teaching. They provide students with the opportunity to explore assessment criteria. This helps them come to terms with the criteria of reference by which their work (and that of their peers) is judged.

The criteria of reference are the set of items against which a piece of work is compared in order to assess its standard. They can be in the form of a mark scheme, a collection of success criteria or work previously completed by other students.

It is possible to use questions as a means to structure peer- and self-assessment. The simplest way to do this is by turning a set of success criteria into questions. Here is an example:

- Explain what the three key terms mean.
- Demonstrate your understanding by giving examples of the three key terms.
- Use the three key terms to explain the source.

These success criteria could become:

- What explanations have been provided of the three key terms?
- How accurate are the explanations?
- What examples has the student given to demonstrate their understanding of the key terms?
- How effective are the examples at showing the student's understanding?
- Has the student explained the source?
- How has the student used the key terms in their explanation?

Plus the obligatory improvement question:

- How might the student improve their work?

By transferring a set of statements into a set of questions, pupils' lives have been made a little easier. The assessments you ask them to make – either of their own work or of that of their peers – are now a series of responses to a series of questions. The greater sense of direction this provides – in contrast to the application of a statement – makes the task more accessible.

One final point to add is that, during peer-assessment, you might like to ask students to set questions for one another instead of targets. Here are some examples of what this might look like:

- How might X be useful in situation Y?
- How might you develop your analysis of X?
- How might your answer have been different if you had given more time to aspect X?

Students can then respond to these questions in writing or in discussion. If the latter option is taken, it will be best to provide some thinking time so that students can digest the question their partner has asked and start to formulate a response.

Chapter Five – Introduction to the exemplar questions

This section of the book contains over 1200 exemplar questions. They are divided as follows:

Chapters six to ten contain approximately 800 questions based on the top five levels of Bloom's Taxonomy of Educational Objectives.

Chapter eleven contains approximately 450 philosophical questions covering all the main areas of the school curriculum.

Chapter twelve contains ninety plenary questions which can be used at the end of any lesson.

Chapter thirteen contains twenty-five questions based on the theme of the past. These are used to demonstrate how you might go about constructing a set of questions around a given theme.

In chapter six to ten, the letter 'X' is used to indicate the subject of a question. This ensures that all the questions remain generic and can therefore be adapted for use with any topic. Here is an example of how to do this:

These are the first three questions from chapter six:

1. **How might an alien identify X?**
2. **What helps you to identify X?**
3. **What might you need to know to successfully identify X?**

Let us imagine that we are teaching a geography lesson on tourism. We could adapt the questions to read:

1. How might an alien identify a tourist destination?
2. What helps you to identify tourist destinations?
3. What might you need to know to successfully identify a tourist destination?

You will note that the questions can be asked of pretty much any subject that we may be teaching about. For example:

1. How might an alien identify a quadratic equation?
2. What helps you to identify bias?
3. What might you need to know to successfully identify a semi-permeable membrane?

By keeping the questions generic, we have been able to provide a bank of challenging, engaging, ready-to-use questions which you can apply in any of your lessons. This will help to save a considerable amount of time.

So, on to the questions!

Chapter Six – Ready-to-use Comprehension Questions

1. Identify

How might an alien identify X?

What helps you to identify X?

What might you need to know to successfully identify X?

What might you need to know to identify specific types of X?

How could you be misled when trying to identify X?

What problems can you imagine for a novice attempting to identify X? How might they avoid or overcome these?

How might you identify X by looking at differences?

How might you decide which things X should go with?

What terms could you use to write about X?

How might it be possible for two strangers who have never met to both identify the same thing as X?

Imagine you were deprived of one/two/three/four senses. Which senses/combinations of senses might allow you to identify X? Why?

What might have to happen to make X unidentifiable?

Who could be most skilled at identifying X and why?

When and where might it be useful to know how to identify X?

Think back to when you couldn't identify X. What might a story of your learning since then be like? What dramas were there? Did failures takes place, or particular successes? What helped you become able to identify X?

What might have to happen for you to be better able to identify X in the future?

How might you break X down into a series of identifiable categories?

What features does X have that help you to identify it?

(Thus – How might the unique combination of these identify X?)

Can you identify the words/images/sounds which might link to X? Why do these things link?

If X was among a selection of similar things, how would you identify it?

How might identifying X be different in different situations?

Could two people identify two separate things as X? How? Why?

Think about the way you have decided X can be identified. How might someone critique this?

Is there a conclusive/definitive way of identifying X?

Is X's identity unique?

When and why might X's identity be subsumed by a broader group identity? (For example, when and why does an oak tree become part of a wood?)

Can you identify X from this list? How were you able to do that?

2. Express

How did X make you feel or think?

What feelings or thoughts did X bring forth in you? Why might this have happened?

What feelings or thoughts might other people express because of X? Why?

Does X make you feel and think different things, or are your feelings and thoughts connected? What are the reasons for this?

How might X have influenced your feelings or thoughts?

How could you use your body to express what X has made you think or feel?

How might you use colour/sound/shape/rhythm/touch to express that which X has made you think or feel?

What might someone think of X? Why?

What thoughts or feelings might person A and person B have about X? How and why might they differ?

How might you express your feelings about X?

What is your opinion of X?

How might you defend your opinion of X?

What reasons, examples or evidence might there be to support your opinion of X?

How might you express X in the context of Y?

How might you use Y as a means to express X?

Why might X lead someone to think or feel certain things?

If X changed, how might your thoughts and feelings about X change as well?

How might a change in Y affect your thoughts and feelings about X?

What might the world be like if no one was allowed to express their thoughts or feelings about X?

What might the world be like if everyone could read other people's thoughts and feelings about X?

How might people think or feel differently about X in different situations?

How could you show how X made you think or feel?

Is there anything which we cannot express ourselves about? If so, why is this? If not, can you think of a situation where we would not in fact be able to express ourselves?

How might you express your thoughts or feelings about X if you were deprived of one/two/three/four senses?

How much of an influence are other factors (for example, past experiences) on your thoughts and feelings about X? How might this be problematic or beneficial?

How might language help you to express your views on X?

How might language hinder you when expressing your views on X?

Where might you be best able to express your views on X? Why?

How might your initial thoughts or feelings about X change following reflection?

3. Describe

How might you describe X?

How might you describe X through actions/words/pictures?

What effect might context have on your description of X?

How might you describe X differently for different audiences? What might be the consequences of this? What might this tell you about the relationship between audience(s) and description?

How might you describe the changes in X over time period Y?

Can you describe how X changes over time?

Can you give a detailed description of X? What might you need to include for your description to be 'detailed'?

How might a description of X be different from a detailed description of X? What might be the consequences, intended or otherwise, of these differences?

How might person A describe X?

How might person A and person B differ in their descriptions of X? What might be the reasons for this?

What effect could motivation or desire Y have on a person's description of X?

Can you describe the constituent parts of X? How does this compare with a general description of X?

How might you describe X to someone deprived of sight/smell/touch/taste/hearing? How might the loss of sense Y affect your ability to describe X?

How might subjective and objective descriptions of X differ? Can *any* description of X be seen as truly objective?

What would you describe as the key features of X?

Can you describe how X makes you feel? Can you describe the connotations X has? Can you describe the associations with X that you have in your mind?

How might you describe the purpose/design/intention/effects/impact of X?

How might you describe the forces which influence X?

How might you describe the relationship X has to its surroundings?

How might a positive description of X differ from a critical description?

How might you describe X so as to take into account conflicting viewpoints?

Where might a description of X prove useful?

Why might it be necessary to describe X?

Who might benefit from a description of X? In what ways would they benefit?

In what circumstances might a description of X prove contentious/useful/vital/helpful/unwieldy? Why?

Before describing X, what criteria do you think would best underpin your description? Why?

How might you best communicate a description of X? Why would this be the best method?

4. Explain

How might you explain X?

How might you explain X person A or group B?

How might you explain X through writing/dance/drama/speaking/symbols?

What might person A need to know in order to explain X?

When might you need to be able to explain X?

When might an explanation of X come in useful? Why? What might this tell us about X?

Who might be able to explain X? Who might make use of an explanation of X? How might they use it?

How might interpreting X be different to explaining it? (And so on with a wide range of alternative verbs)

Why might X be as it is?

What can you tell us about the functions or purpose of X?

Can you explain why you think that?

Can you give a reason for that? What might be a reason for that?

How might you explain your reasoning/actions/ behaviour/choices?

In what circumstances might it be necessary to explain X?

What might be the most effective way of explaining X (...in situation Y/ to person A)?

Considering what you already know, how might you try and explain 'new knowledge X'?

How might X affect your explanation?

New information X appears to contradict/challenge your explanation. How might you explain this problem? How might you alter your explanation to take account of it?

Why might there be different explanations of X? What can we gain/infer/deduce from this? How might these explanations be reconciled? How might the differences/similarities affect our own understanding of X?

How might explaining X help you to understand it?

How might X be explained by theory Y/person A?

How might the effects of X help to explain its purpose/meaning/role/behaviour?

Can you explain what happened? Why might it have happened?

How might you explain the connection between X and Y?

Of the explanations, whose do you find most acceptable? Why?

What might X help you to explain?

What criteria might you use to judge the different explanations of X?

How might you assess an explanation of X?

If you emphasise different factors, how might your explanation of X alter?

When explaining X, what effect might context have?

5. Translate

How might you show X through medium Y?

How might you express X using dance/drama/poetry/algebra?

Can you draw X?

Can you draw your understanding of X?

How might you explain X using different words?

How might you explain X in simpler terms?

How might individuals A and B explain X differently?

If today's learning was turned into a snappy chant, what might it sound like?

Having drawn together the key information, what might it be like as a Haiku?

How might you translate X into form Y?

How might you translate your learning for audience Y?

What might change about X if you were to translate it into medium Y?

What aspects of X will remain most visible if you translate it into medium Y? What does this tell us about X? What does it tell us about medium Y?

Who might find it necessary to translate X, or have it translated for them, in order to aid their understanding? Why?

What essential features of X might be highlighted if we translate it into medium Y?

Where and when might it be useful to translate X into a different form?

Why might translating X into a different form help your own understanding?

Why might translating X into a different form be difficult?

What process might you have to go through in order to translate X into medium/form Y?

How might you translate X using anything you have learnt in maths/science/French (or any other subject)?

What might an equation of your learning look like?

How might you translate X so that it made sense to an alien/animal/plant?

How would you know that a translation made sense? What assumptions would you have to make when translating the material? Why?

How might your understanding of X change when you translate it into medium/form Y? What might this tell us about X, our understanding, or the medium?

Imagine person A was deprived of sense Z. How might you translate X so they were able to understand it?

Imagine you met a group of people with who you could not communicate through language. How might you try to explain X to them?

How might you translate what you have learnt into a form appropriate for audience Y? What form might you choose and why do you think it is appropriate?

How might you explain X using gestures?

Chapter Seven – Ready-to-use Application Questions

1. Apply

How might you use X to deal with situation Y?

In what circumstances might X apply?

When/where might X apply?

What applications of X might there be?

How might two individuals apply X differently?

How might a change in context affect the application of X?

How might the motives or intentions of person A affect how they apply X?

How would you decide whether X can be applied in various situations?

How could you use X to solve problem Y?

If X changed, could it still be applied to Y/in situation Y?

How might group or person A use X to improve their situation?

How might you change X so as to alter its uses? What unintended consequences might your changes cause?

In which situations might you apply X rather than Y (and vice versa)?

Can you develop a rule/set of rules explaining when it is appropriate to use X?

How might you use X in your everyday life?

What uses of X might there be?

Imagine element Z of X was to change, how might this affect the uses of X?

To what extent can X be changed, yet its uses remain the same? What might this tell us about X? What might this tell us about the relationship between X's structure and its use?

What might be the implications of applying X to Y/situation Y?

Could X be applied in situations for which it was not originally intended/in which it is not traditionally used? What might be the results of this?

Why might it be possible to apply X to Y?

Can you construct a table outlining situations where you could apply X, and those where you could not apply it? From this, what conclusions might you be able to draw about X and its uses?

Might there be situations where X does not apply? Do these have something in common? If so, what might this tell us about X?

Imagine someone had not encountered X before. Can you provide guidance that would explain how, when, where and why to apply it?

How much do you need to know about X in order to use it successfully?

How might knowing more about X change how you use it?

Can you think of a situation where X was once useful, but is not anymore?

2. Sketch

Can you sketch X?

If you were to sketch X, what parts would you choose as most important?

What might a general outline of X look like?

How might you sketch different parts of X?

Can you sketch separate parts of X so as to suggest what the whole of X looks like?

What bits of X would a sketch miss out? Would it always be the same? Why?

How might the demands of the audience affect a sketch of X?

Imagine you were asked to include element Y in your sketch of X. How might this alter it? On reflection, what might this tell us about your original sketch?

How might person A and person B sketch X differently?

What might a sketch reveal about the sketcher's beliefs/feelings/thoughts about X? How would you test to see if this was true?

Imagine you had to sketch an outline of X. What would you choose as the most important things to include?

How might a brief account of X differ from a general outline?

What constraints might you come across when sketching an outline of X? How could you overcome these?

How might oral and written sketches of X differ?

Briefly, what is X and how does it work?

How would you ensure accuracy in a general outline of X?

Can you give a brief account of X and explain what parts you think are worthy of further consideration?

How might a sketch of X benefit us/an audience/yourself?

How might a sketch of cause difficulties for us/an audience/yourself?

How would you sketch the main features of X?

How might a brief written account of X and a brief oral account of X differ in emphasis or content?

When might a general outline of X prove most useful?

Why might a brief account of X be better than a full explanation?

How might we judge whether a general outline of X is true or not? Could some bits be true, yet the overall account false?

When dealing with sketches of X, what might we need to be mindful of (compared to when handling all the facts)?

How might a sketch of X lead to misconceptions? What might these misconceptions be? How could you make sure that a sketch of X was clear and accurate?

How might the brief accounts of X by individuals A,B and C be reconciled? Would we want to reconcile them? Why?

3. Choose

Which option could be best for person A? Why?

Which item/tool/concept/idea might best suit the task?

How might you go about choosing from selection X?

What criteria might you use to make a decision about X?

How might your choice(s) about X be different if you used different criteria?

What guidelines would you give someone to help them make choices in situation Y?

Which option might be best in situation Y? Why? How might a change in the situation affect this choice?

How might you approach project X in order to meet the success criteria?

What previous knowledge might be of most use to you here?

Based on theory N, what choices might you make in situations X,Y,Z?

Would you choose theory M or theory N to explain situations X,Y,Z? What are your reasons for your choices?

How might your choices be affected by motives/emotions/rationality/competing claims/morality/opportunity cost?

What might your choice lead you to forgo?

When might your choice be called into question?

If your choice was questioned, how would you explain it?

How might you defend your choice?

What might cause you to alter your choice?

What might be the best form of X in situation Y?

Which option might be most appropriate? Why? On what does this depend? How might change over time/in space/in thought/of people/of culture affect this decision?

What reasons might someone give for opposing your choice?

How might you explain your choice, and the reasons/method behind this, to someone not familiar with the situation/material?

How might the learning help us to choose between X and Y?

What reasoning might you apply to situation X in order to make a decision?

Why might individuals A and B make different choices in situation X?

How might two people use the same knowledge but come to different decisions?

How might you decide what to do in situation X?

What would give you the best opportunity to show your knowledge/skills/understanding?

How might we explain person A's choice in situation X?

Who might choose option X? Why?

4. Demonstrate

How might you demonstrate X?

How might you demonstrate your understanding of X?

How might you demonstrate your understanding of X in situation Y?

How might you demonstrate rule/theory/concept/idea X?

What might you need/need to know in order to demonstrate X?

Can you show me how to use X?

How might you demonstrate X through drama/miming/facial expressions/noises?

How might you try to demonstrate that X is right?

How might you show that X is true?

How might audience Y/context Z affect your ability to demonstrate X?

What features are demonstrated by X?

How might you demonstrate what you have learnt today?

Why/when/where might it be necessary to demonstrate an understanding of X?

How might you use today's learning?

How might you put what you have learnt to practical use?

If you were to be assessed, how might you demonstrate your knowledge/understanding?

What skills/knowledge could you demonstrate in situation X?

Imagine situation/relationship/idea X changed. How would you show that you understood the implications of this change?

Given Y, how might you demonstrate its effects on X?

What skills is person A demonstrating in situation/clip X? What does this information tell us?

What might the existence of X demonstrate?

What might the behaviour/work/speech of person A demonstrate?

Thinking about demonstrating X, how might you break the process down into separate parts? (For example: first unplug the kettle, then fill it with water, then plug it in and turn it on...etc.)

What might be the most effective way of demonstrating X? What are your reasons for this? How might it be affected by who the audience is? How might it be affected by the method/means of communication?

When demonstrating X, what might you expect person A to show/take account of/elucidate?

How much might person A have to demonstrate for you to judge what they are doing as good? Why?

Who might be most capable of demonstrating X? Why? How could you narrow the gap between that person's capabilities and your own? What might their abilities tell you about the nature of X?

How could you demonstrate the connection between X and Y?

Are there things you simply cannot demonstrate? If so, what are they and why can't you demonstrate them? If not, what might this tell us about humans and how they communicate?

5. Solve

How might you solve X?

How might person A try to solve X?

What might you use/need to solve X?

How might you use what we have learnt today to solve X?

How might Y help you to solve X?

What else might you require to solve X? How/why have you reached that conclusion?

How might we solve the problem? What might the ramifications of solving it be? How might they relate to the means by which it is solved?

What might be the answer to /explanation of X?

How might you go about trying to solve problem X? Why would you choose such a method? What alternatives are there? What might these offer which is different from your original idea?

What might explain X?

How might we best deal with X? Why might this be the best way?

What might you need in order to try and solve X?

Under what circumstances, or for who, might it be necessary to solve X? What might this tell us about the nature of X?

What motivation might an individual/group have for solving X?

How might you use reasoning to solve/explain X?

How might you have solved situation X? Would it have differed from what actually happened? If so, why? If not, why?

What different ways might there be to solve X? What might the strengths and limitations of these be? Following on, which would you choose to solve X and why?

Who might be able to solve X? Why?

Having considered our problem, what could you use to solve it?

How might you go about finding an answer to X?

What might today's learning enable us to solve/explain?

How might the problem be solved using X,Y and Z?

On the surface X appears to be a mystery – how might you try to solve it?

What clues might there be leading to a solution for X?

Where might we find a solution to X?

If you were presenting today's problems to next year's class, what would be your advice as to how to go about solving them? Why would you give this advice? How does it link to your own learning?

If part X of the problem changed, how would this affect your solution?

What might you apply to the problem in an effort to solve it?

To what might a solution to X connect? Why?

Chapter Eight – Ready-to-use Analysis Questions

1. Contrast and Comparison

How might X be made more like Y?

How is X different from Y?

What might have caused X to be different to Y?

Why might X and Y have developed differently over time?

How could we distinguish between X and Y?

What could we do to prove that X and Y are different/similar?

Why are X and Y not identical?

Are we able to prove that X is not Y? How?

What would have to happen for X and Y to become more/less similar/different?

How could we categorise X and Y together? How could we categorise X and Y apart?

What elements of X does Y possess (and vice versa)? What then, makes them different?

What analogy might fit both X and Y?

X is to Y, as what is to what? Can you prove it through reasoning?

How does Z's relationship to X and Y differ? Why?

What might Z and X's relationship share with Z and Y's relationship?

How might you draw out the differences/similarities of X and Y for an audience?

What events might affect X but not Y?

How do the elements which make up X and differ from those which make up Y?

How do the origins of X and Y compare?

How could X become Y in N steps?

What conditions might benefit one, but not the other, of X and Y? Why?

Where might X be found, yet not Y? Why?

Where might X and Y both flourish? Why?

How might the users of X and Y differ?

Do X and Y have certain things in common? If so, what are they and why do they have them in common?

What sort of relationship do X and Y have with one another?

How might a world without Y be different from a world without X?

How does the importance of X to human affairs differ to that of Y?

How is human engagement with X and Y different?

What is the cause of the similarities/differences between X and Y?

Can you outline the similarities and differences between X and Y?

2. Examine

How might you plan a thorough examination of X?

What findings might you predict prior to examining X? On what do you base your predictions?

What tools or concepts might you use to examine X?

Which tools/concepts do you feel would be of most use when examining X? Why?

What questions would you try to answer when examining X?

What key question would you use to frame your examination of X? Why?

How might your choice of framing question affect your examination of X?

How might you break X down into manageable segments to examine? What would you need to take into account when doing this? What might be the benefits and pitfalls of reducing X to constituent parts for examination?

How might two examinations of X be different?

Where might be the best place to conduct an examination of X?

How might the environment affect your examination of X?

Who might have previously examined X and how might their findings assist (or hinder) us?

Why might you examine X?

What benefits may there be from working independently/with others on an examination of X? And what potential problems might there be?

What criteria might be useful as a framework for examining X? How might you choose these criteria? How might you apply them? And what might be the effect of all this?

Can an examination of X reveal its true nature or condition? If so, how and why? If not, why not?

How might the results you gain by examining X influence your opinion?

Does the nature or condition of X change over time?

What might be the meaning or purpose of X?

What conclusions might an examination of X lead to? How might you examine whether these are true/valid/reliable?

How might different examinations of X produce different results? What might this tell us about X? What might this tell us about the nature of analysis/the examinations?

In your examination of X, was certain material implicit? Did it rely on you making judgements or inferring meaning? If so, what are the implications of this? If not, can a surface-level examination tell us the true nature or condition of X? Why?

How might you conduct an examination of X that is biased by motive Y? How might knowing this help you to be more objective?

How might X be affected by your examination?

How might examining X affect your understanding of it?

3. Analyse

How might you analyse X?

Can you produce an analysis of X?

Can you produce an analysis of X, paying particular attention to element Y/the influence of Y?

How might X impact on Y?

What is the structure of X?

How might you analyse the structure of X?

How might we analyse the parts that go to make up X?

What (elements) lie(s) at the heart of X?

What (elements) lie(s) behind the functioning/meaning/structure of X?

What might be the meaning of X? What has led you to that conclusion?

What might we conclude from our analysis of X?

How might we subject X to analysis?

What might you expect to find by subjecting X to analysis?

How might analyses of X differ? What implications does this have for our own analysis? What implications does this have for the knowledge of X we may claim to create?

What might we learn by comparing the results of different analyses of X?

When analysing X, what processes/tools/concepts/ideas might be useful? Why?

What method should we use to analyse X? Why? How will we judge if our method has been successful? What might we do if it proves unsuccessful?

What is central/vital/key to X? What is not particularly important to X?

How might X be used? What is it about X that lends itself to such uses?

Who? What? Where? When? Why? How? (5W's + H)

What might X be trying to communicate?

How might motive/bias have influenced X?

What might be the motives of person A?

How might person A have been led to act in this way?

Why did you behave as you did?

What might be the reasoning behind X?

How might X have come to be as it is?

What might be the constituent parts of X?

How might individual/group A's intentions have led to the development of X/situation X? What else may have caused it to develop as it did?

What might have made X like it is?

What influences X internally, what influences it externally? And what influence(s) does X have on other things?

What might be the nature of X? What evidence do you have to support this?

4. Question

Why X? Why X and not Y?

Why might X exist? What might have to happen for X not to exist?

Why might someone ask questions of X?

What questions might we ask about X? Why those particular questions?

What aim should we use to decide what questions to ask about X?

How might a person's motivation/bias/intention affect the questions they ask about X?

Based on your own purpose/motive/aim, what questions would you ask about X?

How might you plan your questioning of X?

What counterfactual questions might you ask about X, in order to offset your original questions?

How could we use questions to achieve a certain result? What might this tell us about the use of questions? How might we use the information to inform our future questioning?

How might the questions asked by person A and person B be different? Why? What might this tell us about the similarities and differences between them?

Would open or closed questions be more helpful to us when analysing X? Why?

How might our questions change if X could respond? (For example, if X was a person we were in contact with, as opposed to a group/idea/object etc.)

How might the situation affect the questions you ask about X? Or the answers you obtain?

What objective questions could we ask about X? What subjective questions could we ask about X? How might these questions be similar or different? What might be the use of asking questions of both types? How would our analysis differ if we favoured one type over another?

What is the overarching question framing your analysis? Why? What might be the pros and cons of beginning with such a question?

Bearing in mind what we have found out about X, how might you formulate a set of questions that someone else could use to reach similar conclusions?

Use everything you know about X to come up with a set of questions that anybody could use to analyse it?

What questions about X might we need to ask as a result of new information Y?

What assumptions do your questions rest on? What assumptions do person A's questions rest on?

Are there any questions about X that cannot be answered? If so, why can they not be answered? Can you imagine how they might be answered in the future?

How valid/reliable/generalizable are the answers to your questions? Why? How might you improve their validity/reliability/generalizability?

Under what circumstances might it be difficult to ask and answer questions about X?

5. Investigate

How might we investigate (the nature of) X?

How might we investigate whether what person A says is true or not?

Why might it be useful to investigate X?

Under what circumstances might it become necessary to investigate X? Why might it become necessary to investigate X?

What motives might people have for investigating X?

How might an investigation of X proceed/work/be structured?

How might an investigation of X be made relevant to our learning?

What could you use to frame your investigation of X?

How might investigating X differ from investigating Y?

How might time, place and context affect your investigation of X?

How might an investigation into a concept be different from an investigation into a physical thing?

What could you use to investigate X?

What might be the benefits of investigating X?

What might you not be allowed to do or use when investigating X?

What problems might you encounter when investigating X?

What difficulties do you think you will have to overcome when planning how to investigate X?

How might the nature of X affect any attempt to investigate it?

What might a successful investigation of X require?

What do you hope to gain by investigating X?

How might different methods of investigation affect what you can find out?

What assumptions might underpin an investigation of X?

What criteria could you use to guide your investigation? Why? Could you use these to judge your results? Why or why not?

What principles will you follow when investigating X? Why?

What question(s) will you seek to answer by investigating X?

How might you check the validity/reliability of any results you generate while investigating X?

If X changed while you were investigating it, how would you respond?

What might be the similarities and differences when investigating X and Y?

How will you judge whether your investigation has been a success or not?

Where might it be easiest to investigate X? Where might it be hardest to investigate X? Where might it be most effective to investigate X?

Chapter Nine – Ready-to-use Synthesis Questions

1. Create

How might X have been created?

How might you create an image/dramatization/story/poem about X?

What might an image/dramatization/story/poem about X be like?

How might X connect to Y? (Can you create a connection between X and Y?)

Could you link X to Y *and* to Z? (Can you create a connection between X, Y *and* Z?)

What conditions are needed for the creation of X? Why? Are there multiple conditions? If so, what might connect these together?

What different stories of X's origin can you tell? How do they differ? Why do they differ? Are there certain things which are common to all stories explaining the creation of X? Why?

What might X help to create?

What could you use X to create?

How might you use X to create Y/something new?

What circumstances might be needed for the creation of X? Why?

If you were to alter condition Y, would X still have been created?

Did the creation of X stifle other possible creations? What might these have looked like? How might the world be different if these, and not X, had been created first?

How might you solve problem X?

What solution(s) can you create for problem X?

Can you create X for situation Y? (For example: What might a constitution for Britain be like? Or: Can you create a constitution (X) for Britain (Y))

What motives might have been behind the creation of X?

Could you create a new/better/more streamlined/more effective/less restrictive version of X?

Can you explain the thinking behind your creation?

What consequences have come from the creation of X?

Can you create an answer to question/problem X?

What processes might be involved in the creation of X? How might these processes interact? What sort of relationship between them is necessary for the creation of X?

Does the creation of X require certain things to happen?

Does the creation of X always lead to certain effects?

Is the creation of X implicated in a chain of cause and effect? Could the creation be explained by indirect factors?

Can you create an image/story/experiment in the style of X?

What do you need to know in order to create something?

2. Design

How might X have been designed?

What alternative designs of X might there be?

What would an alternative to X look like?

How might you design an alternative to X/alternative version of X?

Can you design a solution to problem X?

What might be a solution to X and how would you put this into practice?

What difficulties might you encounter when designing a solution to X?

How might the design of X differ from that of Y?

What constraints might be necessary to encourage a workable design for X?

When designing X, what considerations do you need to take into account?

How might you prioritise the various requirements of the design brief?

Can you design a version of X that takes competing interests/ideas/demands into account?

If the situation changed, how would you design a response to this?

How might person A and person B design different responses to situation Y?

What influence might factor Y have on your design of a solution to problem X?

Why might X have been designed as it is?

What has influenced the design of X? Why has it?

What purposes or intentions do you think the designers of X had in mind?

What unintentional consequences has the design of X led to? What does this tell us about the design of X? What does it tell us about how people are using the design?

How might you design X so that it is future-proof?

Examine X. Use your findings to suggest how it was designed. Why do you think it was designed in this way?

How might you design X so that it is open rather than closed?

How might you redesign X?

What information would be most helpful to someone designing X? How might they get hold of this information? How might it influence their planning?

Look at X. Is there a difference between the design and the reality? Why?

What is the best way to go about designing something? What benefits are there to following a process? What drawbacks are there?

How are designs of X similar and different?

3. Propose

What proposals might you make for situation X?

What solution do you propose for situation X? Why?

What ideas can you propose for altering X?

How might X be altered?

How might we deal with situation X?

What ideas might individuals A and B propose in situation X? Why?

What did you use to make your proposals?

How do you propose to explain your decision?

How might we best explain the actions of person A?

Why might person A have acted as they did? What do you think motivated or caused person A's behaviour?

What theory might explain X? What theory might explain X, Y and Z?

Can you propose an alternative to that which currently exists?

Considering our discussion, what do you propose?

Based on your knowledge and understanding, what do you propose we do?

How might we maintain/analyse/critique/circumvent/challenge/delineate/infer X?

What plan do you have for situation X? How do you plan to do X?

What ideas can you offer as to why X is as it is?

What might have caused X? How? Why?

Who might be responsible for X? Why?

How might person A feel? What might have caused their feelings?

How might person A respond to X? Why might X elicit this response?

How might you improve X?

How might changes to X cause you to alter your proposals?

What factors influenced your proposals? If these were to change, how might your proposals change?

How might we solve problem X? What alternatives are there?

How might the proposal of an idea differ from the proposal of a plan?

Would problem X be better dealt with by a plan or an idea? Why?

If aspect Y of X were to change, what impact might this have on your proposals? Are certain aspects of X more important to your proposal?

Why might your proposal work? Why might it fail? Why might it address the problem? How might it fail to address the problem?

How might you improve your proposition(s)?

Why do you think your proposal will be successful? What evidence/examples/reasons do you have to support your belief?

4. Construct

What theory might explain the information/observations/data?

How might you theorise X from Y?

How might you construct an argument to support your point?

Can you make an argument supporting your point?

Can you construct a meaning for X?

How might you bring X, Y and Z together to form a theory?

Can you construct a new theory which takes X into account?

What might you be able to build using these concepts?

How might these concepts help us to build a model or theory explaining X?

How could we use the concepts we have learnt about to construct a theory of X?

How has person A used observations/data to construct a theory? Do you agree with their theory? Why?

What relationships and concepts are important to theory X?

What might a theory/idea connecting X and Y be like?

What might be the strengths and weaknesses of a theory that tries to explain X, Y and Z?

How can we explain the data/observations?

How could someone go about defending X?

How could someone construct an attack/critique of X?

How can we account for X?

How might person A attempt to incorporate X into their theory?

Could a theory be constructed which challenges X/fits the evidence/gives suggestions for further investigation?

Why might it be possible to construct a theory of X? Why might it not be possible to construct a theory of X?

When/where might it be useful to construct a theory about X?

What might you use to construct a theory about X?

What difficulties might you encounter when trying to theorise X?

Can you construct an answer to X using the data/your knowledge?

What foundations can we construct for our answers?

What would you use to construct an answer to X?

How might individuals A and B construct different theories of X?

What does theory X depend on? How might theory X be proved wrong?

When and how could someone construct an alternative to X? How would they do this? What might make it effective?

How might someone use X, Y and/or Z to build an argument?

5. Hypothesise

How might you explain X?

What might explain X? How might this explanation work?

Who might be able to explain X? Why?

What might happen if X were altered? What might happen if X were altered by means Y? What might happen if X were altered by person A?

What might happen if X was brought into contact with Y?

What hypothesis might fit the facts? What hypothesis might explain X?

What might happen in situation X? Why – what has led you to such a hypothesis?

Can you think of a hypothesis which accounts for X, Y and Z?

Why might X be as it is?

How might you improve X? Why would what you have suggested be an improvement?

What might make X better or worse? Why?

How might you explain X? Given new information Y, how might your hypothesis about X alter?

How could you test your hypothesis about X?

How could X be different?

Why/where could X be different?

Who might want to explain X? Why?

How might X be explained? How might X be explained using Y/by person A?

What might be the best course of action for achieving X? Why?

What assumptions does your hypothesis rest on?

How might your hypothesis influence how you look at X?

How could someone attempt to falsify your hypothesis?

How might a change in motivation influence your hypothesis?

How many different hypotheses might possibly explain X? What does this tell us about X? What does it tell us about proposing hypotheses?

Which hypothesis about X do you think is most likely to prove correct? Why?

How might you simplify your hypothesis?

What information do you need to prove or disprove your hypothesis?

What information might lead you to alter your hypothesis? Why? What changes will you make?

How might you develop a hypothesis that explains X?

Will you hypothesis about X be true in every situation? How could you test this?

Why might someone agree or disagree with your hypothesis about X?

How might you test your hypothesis?

Chapter Ten – Ready-to-use Evaluation Questions

1. Assess

How might we assess X?

What assessments of X can you make?

What is the likelihood of X doing/exhibiting behaviour Y?

How might X be improved? Why? What benefits would this bring and for who?

How important is X in the context of Y?

What value might we place on X? How might this change in different circumstances?

What internal changes could alter the value of X?

What external changes might alter the value of X?

When might X have the greatest value for person A?

In what contexts would X prove reliable or valid?

How might we assess the validity or reliability of X?

What criteria could you use to assess X? Why? How might different criteria lead to different assessments?

How might you assess X in reference to Y or Z?

How might person A and person B come to different assessments of X?

Could a set of criteria be developed that resulted in uniform assessments of X no matter who was assessing it? Why?

How might we assess whether or not X can be classed as belonging to category Y?

What would we need to know in order to confidently assess X?

What is X? How do you know? What thinking led you to that assessment?

How might we assess the impact of X on Y?

What chances are there for X being successful/failing? How might these chances be enhanced or degraded?

Do the strengths of X outweigh the benefits? Why?

If you could recreate X from scratch, what might you do differently? If nothing, why then has X proved successful?

What aspects of X are the most significant? Why?

How and why might person A and person B think differently about X?

Why might X exist?

What might be the purpose of X?

Consider what you know about the world. How might X, or the way X is used, change in the future? Why?

What circumstances might be most conducive to the success of X?

What qualities does X possess that would enable it to flourish/succeed in situation Y?

2. Argue

What arguments could you make in favour of X?

What arguments could you make against X?

What arguments might have been put forward in order to bring X about?

What arguments might have been put forward in an attempt to prevent X coming into existence?

Who or what might argue in favour of X? Why?

Who or what might argue against X? Why?

Consider the arguments for and against X, how do they compare? Are there things which are common to both? Do they share assumptions? Or, do they make different assumptions? In either case, what are the implications for the arguments?

On what assumptions does argument X rely?

What motives might the people proposing argument X have?

How could you rebut the arguments made against X?

How might we test argument X?

How might we falsify argument X?

What arguments about X might person A's motives lead them to make?

What might you need to know and understand about X in order to successfully argue for or against it?

How could you support your claims about X?

What evidence, examples or reasons could be used in support X?

What might be the strengths and weaknesses of argument X? Why might this be so? What might it tell us about the argument more generally?

Why might argument X be convincing?

Why might individuals or groups accept that argument X is valid? What does this tells us about those individuals or groups? What might it tell us about the motivations of those people who propose argument X?

In what circumstances might argument X prove successful? Why?

How might you support what you have just said?

Why might the evidence support the argument?

On what reasoning does argument X rely?

What steps might someone go through to build an argument around X?

What emotions or shared meanings is argument X invoking?

If the premises changed, how would this affect your argument?

What new evidence could disprove argument X?

How could you maintain your position in situation Y?

3. Justify

How might you justify X?

Who might seek to justify X?

How might person A justify their opinion/belief/proposal? Why might they try to justify it? What might motivate them to justify X? What factors might influence their decision to justify X? What might influence the manner in which they justify X?

When might you be able to justify X? What changes will make this no longer appropriate?

When, or why, might someone be unable to justify X?

How might you use evidence or reasoning to support your argument?

What justification is there for accepting that X is true?

How might you justify your position in the face of argument X? How might you justify your argument to person A or group B?

What impact might evidence X have on your defence of position Y?

Considering the strengths and weaknesses of the claims, which do you believe to be most justified in the circumstances?

How might you assess the justifications put forward for position X?

How might you justify a change to/maintenance of the status quo?

When could the use of X be justified?

Where might the use of X be justified?

In what circumstances might you try to justify X?

How might you prove that X is either right or reasonable?

Is there any evidence to justify X? Could you manufacture evidence to justify X? How?

What underpins your justification? What underpins person A's justification?

Can you critique person A's justification by analysing the logical/deductive/semantic/theoretical grounds on which it is based?

How has person A tried to justify their reasoning/position/actions?

To what, or to who, does person A appeal when justifying their position?

How might an emotional justification of X be different from a rational justification?

How might you justify X without using language/certain words/gesticulations/empirical evidence/logic?

How might religious and scientific/historical and philosophical/social and cultural justifications differ?

What assumptions might underlie the justification of X?

What might be the ethical/political/social/theoretical consequences of justifying X?

How might person A attempt to justify the actions of person B or group C? Why might they do this?

How might person A try to persuade other people that their justification is valid?

How can we test whether your justification of X is true or not?

4. Judge

What is your opinion of X? Why? What has led you to that view? What assumptions underpin it? How has your opinion been influenced by X/preconceptions/prior knowledge?

Would X or Y be better/more appropriate/more useful in situation Z?

How can we judge X?

How might person A judge X? How and why might this judgement differ from that of person B?

How might context affect someone's judgement of X?

Who might need/desire/wish to judge X?

What judgements can we make about X?

Based on the criteria, what is your opinion of X? Why?

What criteria can you use to judge X?

What is your opinion of X? On what criteria is your judgement based?

What might make it possible to judge X? Could X be judged differently according to different assumptions/demands/ideas?

What type of judgement might be of most use in situation X? Why?

Following new information Y, has your opinion of X altered? Why?

On what do your opinions about X rest? Are there motives/principles/intuitions/reasons guiding your judgements? If so, why are these important? On analysis, *are they important*?

What might be the value of X to person A/in situation B?

What are your thoughts about X?

Why might X be better than Y? And vice versa? In your opinion, which is better? Why? Will this always be the case?

Which of these ideas might be better in situation X/for group Y?

How effective is X? How have you come to that judgement? How else might we judge the effectiveness of X? What consequences does this have for our understanding of X?

What is good/bad/useful/tasteless about X? Why?

Having heard all the evidence, what is your opinion of X? How does your opinion link to the evidence? Does the evidence structure/support/negate it?

In your opinion, how might X be improved/altered/remade? What led you to such a judgement? On making your thinking clearer, does your opinion alter? Why?

X or Y? For what reasons? And these reasons – what underpins them? What work might concepts be doing in your thinking? If you were to judge the validity of your concepts, might this lead you to alter your original view? Why?

Is X justified? Why?

How might you come to form an opinion? What concepts or processes might be influential in your thinking?

Where or when might someone's judgement of X alter?

How would you prioritise the various criteria when making a judgement about X?

5. Critique

How might you critique X?

Can you offer us a critique of X?

How might someone critically evaluate X?

What criticisms of X are there?

How might someone go about criticising X?

What are the strengths and weaknesses of X?

Thinking critically, what is your final judgement about X?

How might person A critique X? How might this differ from your own critique? How might you explain this difference?

What relationship might there be between a person's motivation/purpose/aims and their critique of X?

How might someone use their critique of X? How might you use someone else's critique of X?

What rules do people follow when critiquing something? Do these differ depending on what is being critiqued?

What problems might arise from X? What problems might X entail? How might X be a problem? What might X make difficult?

What faults or difficulties might someone find with X?

How useful might X be? Why?

What use might X be in situation Y? Why?

What limitations does X have?

What are the causes of X's limitations?

What might be the positives and negatives/pros and cons of X?

Having analysed the positives and negatives of X, what is your opinion of it?

What criticisms of X might person A put forward?

How might someone use Y to critique X?

On what might a critique of X rely?

What do you need to know or understand in order for your critique of X to be effective?

On what criteria does your critique of X rely? How might these direct your thinking on the issue?

What could you use to critique X?

What might a critique of X entail?

On what grounds might we be able to go ahead with a critique of X?

Why might X prove difficult to critique? What, if anything, might allow us to successfully critique X?

How or why might something prove to be difficult to critique? How or why might person A struggle to critique X?

Why bother to critique X?

Chapter Eleven – Ready-to-use Philosophical Subject-Specific Questions

The questions which follow cover each main area of the school curriculum. They are philosophical, meaning they are about concepts, categories and big ideas. You can use them to stretch and challenge the thinking of all your students.

1. Art

What is art?

Can we define art?

Can art be fully explained?

How do people make aesthetic judgements?

What does it mean for a work of art to be described as 'good' or 'bad'?

On what do we base our judgements about art?

Is it possible to judge a work of art?

Of what are responses to art composed?

Is there an ultimate (discoverable) standard in aesthetics?

Is all artistic judgement culturally specific?

Can artistic judgement be learnt? If so, or if not, what might be the consequences of this?

What role does feeling play in a person's experience of art?

Does art have to be 'experienced'? If so, what does this mean? If not, why not?

Where does art come from?

Is all aesthetic judgement ultimately the expression of individual feeling?

Is form more important than content?

How can form and content be successfully married?

How do we *know* that something is art? (*Can* we know that something is art?)

Can art express or subvert power?

Does the deprivation of one or more senses lead to a fundamentally different conception of art?

How does art relate to reality?

Is art an extension of reality, a description of it, or a reflection of it? (Or something else entirely?)

Does a work of art require an audience in order for it to be a work of art? What are the consequences of this?

How do property rights affect art?

Is art an expression of an individual or is it an expression of something beyond them?

Do artists have moral responsibilities to society?

Should any society help artists to develop?

Can art express truth? If so, what is the nature of this truth?

How might art fulfil an ethical role in people's lives?

2. Business Studies/Economics

Is self-interest a good motive?

Does the pursuit of more, be it profit, goods etc. lead to personal fulfilment?

How should wealth be distributed in society?

Should governments intervene in markets?

Why should people obey government regulations (nationally, locally and internationally)?

What is the relationship between economics and morality?

Is it right to separate moral considerations from economic ones?

Do markets exist? If yes, how might this be proved? If no, what then is being talked about?

To what extent are individuals rational?

Do people understand their own motives for acting/making decisions?

How far should property rights extend over the Earth's resources (For example: To the atmosphere? To rainfall?)

Does custom justify property rights? If so, why? If not, what are the consequences of this?

What is the aim of economics?

How should owners of firms prioritise the interests of themselves, others and society?

Regarding businesses, what are the interests of owners, of society, of workers and of others?

Do people have the right to pursue economic opportunities as they see fit?

What justification is there for governments limiting the range of things firms and individuals can do?

Are taxes paid by consent or because of the threat of force?

How does culture affect economic behaviour and economic relationships? What are the consequences of this for discussions about economics?

Is it morally right to separate people's economic considerations from the rest of their lives?

Does money exist, or is it just a confidence trick?

What role should the state have in an economy?

What is the relationship between money and power?

Does a strong economy need a high level of trust?

Are consumers responsible to those people involved in producing goods and services?

Is lending money morally acceptable?

Can we rely on business and economic forecasts? Why?

3. Citizenship

Do individuals have a responsibility to those less fortunate than themselves?

Does society exist?

How would you prioritise the interests of the individual, the family, the community, society, and the globe? What are the consequences of this?

What justification is there for accepting human rights?

Why should anyone obey anyone else?

Can the demands for freedom and for security be satisfactorily reconciled? Which is more important – freedom or security?

Do people have a duty to get involved in politics?

What is politics?

How is power distributed in society?

What underpins the distribution of power in society?

Is there such a thing as a 'self'? If so, of what is it constituted and how can it be known? If not, then what do we mean when we talk about it?

On what foundations does identity depend?

How can anything other than an individual (for example, an institution or a country) have an identity?

Should the government make decisions based on the idea of maximizing happiness? If so, why? If not, what are the alternatives?

How can laws (or the rule of law) be justified? (If by custom – is this coherent? If by force – is this right? If by reason – is this contingent?)

Is the state ever justified in using force? Is it ever justified in killing individuals?

Is the idea of human rights enough for describing how we should act towards one another?

Is it ever right to use violence to achieve a goal?

Are protests or campaigns acceptable if they threaten the safety or livelihood of other people?

Is democracy 'the best' form of government?

Do we have duties towards animals/the environment/unborn humans?

Do animals/the environment/unborn humans have rights?

Can the demands of justice and of caring for others be reconciled? If so, how? If not, which should be prioritised and why?

Is justice something we know innately, or through experience?

What makes a society 'good'?

4. Design and Technology

What does it mean to describe a design as 'good' or 'bad'?

How can something be a 'good design'?

Are the properties we attribute to the same materials identical? (For example: Is my blue your blue?) If so, can this be proved?

Do designers have ethical responsibilities to society?

To what extent are designers responsible for the outcomes of their actions? (For example: The designer of propaganda)

When we say a design is 'pleasing', what do we mean?

Could technology ever replicate the experience of humans?

Does technology extend the experience of humans?

Should we pursue the development of new technology for its own sake, regardless of the potential results?

Can we know the effects new technology might have on us or on our society?

Is a computer like a brain?

How can we know what properties different materials have?

Does all design have to have a purpose to it?

Did God design the universe?

Is the physical world like a big machine? Why?

What does someone have to have to be called a craftsman?

Should intellectual property rights be enforced? Why and by who?

What does it mean to *be* creative?

Are our minds limited or changed by the technology we use?

Is technology morally neutral?

What are the limits of design?

Should design aim for practicality or aesthetic perfection?

What does it mean for something to be described as 'useful'?

Should we attribute value to technology? Why?

Is it better to design systems for humans or to allow for organic development?

How might the craftsman's knowledge of materials affect his understanding of the physical world?

Is it possible to design something without a purpose?

What values should the designer prioritise? Why?

Are there areas of human life where technology should not tread? (For example: Genetic engineering)

5. Drama

Does drama have a negative effect on the morality and beliefs of people who watch or participate in it?

Should a writer or director try to challenge the beliefs of the audience?

Is it right to commercialise artistic work?

Should plays be censored for younger audiences?

Is it right to set up a boundary between audience and performers?

Does drama provide us with truth? If so, what type of truth?

Is it morally justifiable to portray living people on stage? What about God?

How might someone's experience of drama affect how they think and act?

Can the use of drama for political purposes be justified?

Do actors know a character or a text? If so, what type of knowledge do they possess?

Should a skilled actor use their abilities for personal gain?

Is acting lying? If not, what is it? If so, what then does it tell us about the status of lying?

What does it mean to describe a play as 'good'?

Does drama have a permanent set of criteria against which it is judged, or are these culturally and historically specific? Either way, what are the consequences of this for the people involved and for the dramatic works themselves?

Is drama a representation of reality? Or, is it a representation of ideas in the minds of individuals (author, director, actors, audience)?

Is it ever right to trick an audience? What about tricking an actor?

Is it right to use dramatic concepts and categories when talking about things which are outside of the theatre (For example: Everyday life, photographs and rituals)? Why?

Can drama reveal moral truths?

Can drama be used to obscure or suppress truth? Should it ever be used in this way?

Is it possible to neuter language so that it does not contain any drama?

How does drama affect people's experience of reality?

Can our understanding of historical plays ever escape the contemporary concepts and categories that we have?

What do we mean when we describe a reproduction as 'faithful'?

Can anyone successfully communicate the experience of acting?

Is drama likely to mislead? Should we to teach young people how to resist it?

Does drama turn people away from reality? If so, so what? If not, why not?

6. English

Is literature a mirror to life?

What do we mean when we describe a novel or a poem as 'good'?

Against what aesthetic standards are works of literature or poetry judged?

Can any aesthetic judgement of literature or poetry stand up to interrogation? (Can it be ultimately justified?)

Can fiction provide us with true knowledge?

What are the strengths and limitations of trying to come to terms with experience subjectively?

To what does literature or poetry refer? Is it things in the world, or things in the author's mind?

Where are ideas? Do they persist? Do they make up the reality we experience?

Does language refer to external objects? Is this true of all language?

What determines the coherence/legitimacy of a proposition?

Why is it that certain words or phrases can compel changes in the world? (For example: Stop! Or, 'With these words I thee wed')

Is it possible to have a private language?

Is there a logical basis to language?

What does a word such as 'good' or 'game' mean? What are the consequences for our understanding of language? What are the consequences for how we go about defining words?

How does language influence our experience and understanding of reality?

Is the reality we experience a consequence of the words we possess? Is reality an interpretation limited by the words we possess?

Should works of literature be subject to intellectual property rights? Why?

Is it wrong to use language duplicitously?

Could we ever know, definitively, if someone was using language duplicitously?

Are there ethical problems implicit in the teaching of rhetoric and persuasive language?

Should authors aim at some conception of truth? Why?

Do authors have a moral responsibility to their subject/society/posterity?

Is language an impediment to true knowledge? Is language an impediment to knowledge of God?

Can there be knowledge without (or before) language?

Is political power implicit in discourse? What are the consequences of this?

Is language neutral?

Does a society have a moral responsibility to teach its young how language can be manipulated?

Should there be censorship? On what grounds?

7. Geography

Does the world have a designer?

Can we prove how the world came to be as it is?

What can we know and prove about the physical environment?

What makes a tourist destination desirable or pleasing? Is this measurable? Is it an objective standard?

Do tourists have an ethical responsibility when choosing their holiday? What about when they use resources?

Can a holiday be ethically justified, given that many people all over the world cannot go on one?

Should people not go to countries where human rights are being abused?

Is it morally justifiable for the rich to holiday in places where there is great poverty?

To what extent does our description of the physical world affect how we interact with it?

Does geology disprove the existence of God?

Is it right to put controls on population growth?

Does the environment influence people's experiences of reality?

What makes a landscape beautiful?

Can any description of natural beauty hold across time and in different cultures?

Does the environment have rights?

Is it right to turn the natural world into property?

Does development necessarily require an increase in individual freedom?

Should all countries try to pursue economic growth?

Do MEDCs have a duty to help LEDCs? Should they hinder their own growth to help LEDCs grow quicker?

On what grounds, or using what criteria, should governments make economic decisions?

Should government economic policy be influenced by ideas of right and wrong? If so, who's right and wrong?

What should be on a map and what should have greater prominence? How might this affect our notions of reality? How might it reflect our ethical beliefs?

If we used knowledge like an atlas – for example, by having different maps for different areas of thought or ways of thinking – what might be the consequences?

Should all land be open access? If so, why? If not, why not? And, what land should be open access?

The coast is constantly eroding and tectonic plates are forever moving. Does this mean that our maps are false? Does it mean that a perfect map could never be made?

What does the inside of a mountain feel like?

8. History

To whom does the past belong?

What can we know of the past?

What knowledge about the past can we have? How do we know that it is true knowledge?

Do historians have moral duties to society/their subject/the past?

Does the past exist? Can we prove it either way?

How might history be used for political ends? Can the past be misused? Why?

What does it mean to *say* history has been misused? What might this tell us about our conceptions of truth?

What is the relationship between history and myth? How does this show itself in our understanding of the world?

Can the past be used for moral training in the present? Should it be used in this way?

Does history have a purpose? Is history a moral problem?

Is history art or science? Is it *sui generis?*

Is all description interpretation? If not, can this be proved? If yes, what are the consequences for studying history?

Does history privilege certain groups? If so, what are the political and ethical consequences of this?

Do ideas remain the same over time, or are they forever tied to a particular period?

What should be memorialised? Why? Who should decide?

Do individuals have an obligation to find out about the past before they speak about it?

Can history ever be definitive? Why? What are the consequences of your answer for our ideas about truth?

How might we judge the 'truth' of a source?

Is there a 'proper' way to study the past? What might be the ethical and political implications of this?

Is it right to claim the past for the purposes of the present?

Should certain aspects of the past be suppressed for 'the greater good'?

Do political systems rely on a narrative of origins/progress for legitimacy?

Can tradition be used as a justification?

Is history a unified flow of experience? Is there a distinct, knowable, 'past reality'?

Does historical explanation tell us about the truth of the past? Can there be a true representation of the past?

Can the past be used to legitimise actions? If so, can it be used to legitimise anything that has been done? Why?

Do different types of history different types of knowledge available to us?

How might the historian's own concepts and categories order or influence their descriptions and interpretations of the past?

When writing history, should historians question whether the choices they are making are right or wrong?

Is there cause and effect in history? Can this be proven either way?

9. Information Communication Technology (ICT)

Should the internet be censored?

Can there be (should there be) property rights on the internet?

Can computers replicate human experience?

Could a computer ever feel or think?

Does ICT alter our understanding or interpretation of reality and experience?

Is information a useful metaphor for explaining our interaction with the world?

Is it ever right to hack into another computer?

Can the release of a computer virus be morally justified?

Should governments use computers to survey their populations?

Is technology morally neutral?

Can something generated using a computer ever match traditional standards of beauty?

Is information stored in binary code known in the same way as something stored within a person's memory?

Does ICT undermine the power and authority of the state?

Is it right to store sensitive information in electronic form?

Does the internet exist? If so, where is it? If not, then what do we refer to when we say 'the internet'?

What is the status of information presented to us on computers? Does it exist?

How might the development and retail of computer software influence our experience of the world?

Is there a qualitative difference between digital and analogue information? If so, what are the consequences for an individual who uses one over the other?

Is it morally justifiable to replace a person with a computer, for example, in the workplace?

Who has authority over the internet?

Should computers and associated materials be made in a sustainable fashion?

Is it morally wrong for a computer game to replicate morally evil acts?

Could robots ever be made that would be classed as humans?

Should the state ever be allowed to access private e-mails?

Some components for computers may be mined in conditions antithetical to human rights and the welfare of those involved. Do consumers have a responsibility to be aware of (and act upon) such things?

Can computer modelling give us knowledge of the future?

What are the limits to the knowledge we can gain using ICT?

10. Maths

To what does zero refer?

Can 'nothing' exist?

Can mathematical laws be known independently of experience?

Is it just to abstract people into numbers?

Does society have a duty to teach people about the validity and reliability of statistics?

Can any statistical measure claim to be objective?

Given the limitations of our knowledge of the world, can any statistic be said to be reliable and/or valid?

Is it right to manipulate statistics to support an argument? How would you define manipulation?

Do numbers refer to things, ideas, relations or something else?

How far can we use logic to describe the world?

Does the division of things into equal parts suggest an idea of justice which is independent of human thought?

How might thinking in binary influence someone's conception of the world?

Should mathematics, and logic, be seen as a higher form of knowledge?

Are mathematics and logic privileged above other types of knowledge by virtue of their perfectibility?

Can 'pure mathematics' be justified as a good use of a person's time and resources?

Are all things measurable? What is the consequence of this for our views of measurement?

How might mathematics (for example measurement and abstraction) be used for political purposes?

Should politicians and administrators be allowed to treat individuals as things (through the use of numbers and abstraction)?

Many mathematical truths appear to hold for all time. What consequences might this have for our descriptions of reality? What about for the validity of our perceptions?

Is it desirable for everybody in a society to study maths? Why?

Do mathematical truths prove the existence of God or a creator?

What makes a sequence, progression, equation and so on aesthetically pleasing?

Is mathematical knowledge politically and ethically neutral?

To what does infinity refer?

Are there different types of infinity?

If infinity and zero cannot be demonstrated empirically, what might be the consequences for our understanding of reality?

How much of maths is imaginary? Does this matter?

11. Modern Foreign Languages

Does language influence a person's conception of the world?

How might being multilingual affect a person's understanding of reality (or, of language)?

Is a translator responsible for being truthful?

Should governments enforce the learning of foreign languages?

If so, is it right to do this for certain reasons – for example, to decrease xenophobic sentiment; or to improve the country's trade position?

Can a translation ever convey the meaning of the original?

If someone learns a foreign language, is their understanding limited by their own culture or upbringing?

Is it right to divorce the learning of a language from the culture in which that language developed?

Do different languages represent qualitatively different experiences of reality?

Are the cultures in which languages exist knowable by those who are outside?

What do we mean when we use the word 'language'?

Can a concept or idea present in one language but not in another be translated?

Should learners be taught how rhetoric and persuasion work in the language they are learning?

Is it justifiable to trick students in order to help them learn a new language?

How does political power manifest itself in language? (For example: What type of language is learnt? E.g. the 'Queen's English')

Do language teachers have a responsibility to the country whose language they teach?

Would it be justifiable for a translator to deceive one party if they believed it was for a greater good?

Can we know what we claim to know in our language, in another language? Would it be possible to prove this?

Can we prove that two individuals communicating through translation know what it is they are speaking about?

Are any aspects of language untranslatable? If so, what might be the consequences of this (particularly for the status of knowledge)?

Is language a technology? If so, what influence does it have on people's perceptions of the world?

How do orality and literacy differ? Do they offer us qualitatively different ways of knowing about the world?

Can someone come to know standards of taste or judgement through the learning of a language?

Should there be any moral or political considerations when deciding what learners are to be taught about a new language?

Is learning a dead language a waste of time?

Can the preservation of a language through making it a compulsory subject be justified?

What is the purpose of schoolchildren learning foreign languages?

12. Physical Education

Is it justifiable to cheat in order to gain an advantage for yourself or for your team?

What is a 'game'?

What do we mean when we use the word 'cheat'?

Do we have an ethical obligation to look after our bodies?

What is the nature of a sportsperson's knowledge about their sport? Can it be conveyed?

To what does the notion of 'flow' refer? (As in, being in the flow)

Why is one pass, shot, save and so on described as good, but another not?

On what grounds are some sporting actions or pieces of play defined as aesthetically pleasing?

Can someone possess physical knowledge (before or beyond language)? If so, can we prove they possess this? If not, what then is the knowledge that sportspeople possess?

Is it useful to think of the body as a machine? Why? What might be the consequences of this view?

Is mechanism a useful metaphor for describing the body? Why? What might be the consequences of this view?

What are the benefits and limitations of employing science as a means to know about sport?

How should responsibility be divided up in a team?

How should blame and praise be distributed in a team?

Is competition problematic when it becomes a part of teaching and learning?

Should sport be valued by society? Why, and to what ends?

Can any referee or umpire be truly objective?

How do reason and emotion manifest themselves in the thinking and motivations of sportspeople?

Should an individual athlete submit to the authority of a coach?

Should sportspeople submit to the authority of an umpire or referee? Why? What is the justification?

Does physical fitness need to have an end, or can it be an end in itself?

How much should someone be willing to sacrifice for the good of the team? What about for the possibility of future success?

What role should the government play in the funding and governance of sport? Why?

What justification is there for following the rules of a sport or a game?

Could performance-enhancing drug-taking ever be justified?

If an athlete took performance-enhancing drugs but was never discovered, is there a problem?

Should sports that involve physical violence to other humans (or animals) be allowed?

Is winning more important than anything else?

13. PSHE

What is an individual?

Do we possess a unified self?

Do we change over time or in different situations? What are the consequences of this for our knowledge of our self and other people's experience of us?

What is the right thing to do?

Should you be consistent in matters of morality? Why?

What do we mean when we use the word 'healthy'?

Do we have jurisdiction over our own bodies?

To what extent should individuals be allowed to decide matters concerning themselves? (For example: abortion, euthanasia and suicide)

Do we have a duty towards others?

Is self-interest a legitimate way to make decisions?

When we speak of self-interest, what do we mean? Is it happiness, pleasure, virtue or something else?

Do we have a responsibility towards our bodies?

Is any area of life exempt from politics? Is the personal political?

Does the state have an obligation to involve itself in private matters?

Should individuals be left alone by the state? Why and to what extent?

What do we mean when we describe something as 'private'?

What is love?

Do we have moral responsibilities towards sexual partners? If so, what are they?

Is sex a distinct area of life, or should we consider it as a part of our interpersonal relationships?

What should the state provide in terms of public health? Should contraception, sanitary towels, dementia care and so on be provided for free?

Can any moral position be ultimately justified? Why?

Why do people act as they do? What aims, motivations, reasons and desires cause behaviour? Can behaviour be adequately explained by the notion of cause and effect?

How might someone's upbringing, education, social position and so on affect their understanding and interpretation of the world?

Can we have knowledge of ourselves? If so, how?

Can we share knowledge of ourselves with other people?

14. Religious Studies

Does God exist?

Can we prove the existence, or non-existence of God?

Is the universe designed? Does the universe have a creator? Can this be proved?

Do miracles prove the existence of God?

Why should anyone follow the rules of a religion?

What do we mean when we use the term 'religion'?

Is there a meaning to life? Does life or the universe have a purpose? What might be the consequences of answering these questions?

Is revelation a form of knowledge?

Can God be known?

What justification is there for faith?

Does science undermine the legitimacy of religious thought or knowledge?

Could someone use religious rules as guidance in every situation they face?

Do humans have free will?

Should humans exercise their free will if it is against the word or laws of God? If the answer is no, can humans be said to have free will? If the answer is yes, can God be said to be all-powerful?

Why is there evil in the world? (If God is all-powerful and all-good, then why does evil exist?)

What is the nature of God?

What is the right thing to do?

Does revelation, faith or God offer a legitimate basis, an ultimate foundation, for ethical judgements?

Should religion be a part of politics?

Do religious believers have duties towards others? If so, what are these duties and what justifies them?

Should religious believers involve themselves in politics?

How might religious belief influence someone's understanding or beliefs about physical reality?

Does heaven exist? Can this be proven?

What is the nature of religious knowledge?

Should religious belief be tolerated in a secular society? Should any religions be banned?

Can any society be said to be truly secular?

15. Science

What is the nature of scientific knowledge?

Can induction provide us with ultimate laws?

Does science occupy a privileged position in Western society? If so, what might be the consequences of this?

What are the limitations of scientific explanation?

Can the model of mathematics, and by extension physics, be applied throughout science? If yes, with what justification? If no, what are the consequences for scientific ways of knowing?

Is any area of science a more powerful explanation of the natural world than any other? (For example: Is physics a better way of knowing than chemistry?) Why?

What can we know about the physical world and how is this knowledge justified?

Bearing in mind the history of scientific revolutions, should we treat all scientific knowledge as provisional?

How do quantitative and qualitative ways of knowing differ?

Does science disprove the existence of God?

Darwin's theory of evolution is not definitively proven. Does this mean we should teach other theories alongside it?

Are scientists responsible for the effects of their discoveries?

Should scientists consider the ethical implications of what they do?

Is it ethically justifiable for scientists to take employment with companies who will not disclose how they will use research discoveries?

Is scientific description interpretation? (For example: Are words like 'atom' and 'gene' actually metaphors?)

Can anything be completely objective?

What ethical issues might there be if we privilege objective over subjective knowledge?

How do scientific concepts and categories affect our language?

Do humans have free will, or are our actions determined?

What is the relationship between cause and effect? Can such a relationship be proven?

Can we rely on the information we receive through senses?

Can it be proven that materials have properties (or even exist!) independent of observation?

Is it better to produce a seemingly effective theory that discounts anomalies or to scrupulously collate all possible data?

Can science lead humans to knowledge of everything there is to know?

How do the concepts and categories of science affect how we think?

Chapter Twelve – 90 Ready-to-use Plenary Questions

This chapter contains ninety questions which you can use as plenaries. All are generic, referring to the lesson or to the learning. Therefore, they can all be used regardless of what has gone before.

1. What have you learnt today?
2. What is the most important thing you have learnt today?
3. What do you know now, that you did not know at the start of the lesson?
4. How has your understanding changed as a result of the lesson?
5. What three things have you learnt today?
6. What would you choose as the key thing you have learnt today? Why?
7. What do you want to know as a result of what we have learnt today?
8. What can you do now that you could not do at the start of the lesson?
9. How has today's lesson changed you knowledge or understanding?
10. What questions do you have, based on today's lesson?
11. Why do you think we have studied what we have studied this lesson?
12. How might you change today's lesson for future students? Why?
13. How might you use your learning from today's lesson in the future?
14. What has been the purpose of today's lesson?

15. How might you use what you have learnt today?
16. If you were going to teach this lesson to younger students, what would you identify as the key things they would need to know?
17. Based on what we have learnt today, what do you think we should study next? Why?
18. Where might you make use of the learning you have done today?
19. Under what circumstances, or for what reason, might we need to use today's learning?
20. How might you test one of your peers to see what they have learnt today?
21. How might you explain what you have learnt today to your parents?
22. How might you explain what you have learnt today to an alien?
23. How might you explain what you have learnt today to someone younger than yourself?
24. What connections can you make between today's learning and what we have studied previously?
25. How does today's learning connect to what you already know?
26. How might today's lesson have been different? What might have been the result of this?
27. How might we have learnt the same things, but in a different way?
28. Who might use what we have learnt today in their daily lives?
29. How have you worked today? Why?
30. How might you improve your learning next lesson?
31. What have been the strengths and weaknesses of this lesson?

32. What skills have you used during this lesson?

33. What skills have you improved during the lesson? How have you improved them?

34. What knowledge have you gained this lesson?

35. How might you use the knowledge you have gained in this lesson in the future?

36. How have you interacted with your peers during this lesson?

37. What strengths and weaknesses have you seen in yourself this lesson?

38. What changes might you make next lesson to how you work?

39. How has today's lesson made you feel?

40. To what extent do you feel you have engaged with the lesson today? Why?

41. To what extent do you feel you have learnt in today's lesson? Why?

42. How have you learnt this lesson?

43. In what way(s) has your mind been changed by today's lesson?

44. If you were to go back in time and start today's lesson again, what would you change and why?

45. How could you have done things differently this lesson? What affect might this have had?

46. How did you feel at the beginning, middle and end of the lesson?

47. How have you used you existing skills and knowledge in today's lesson?

48. What have you done well this lesson and why?

49. Can you write a poem about what you have learnt today?

50. Can you create a short story based on today's lesson?

51. Can you write a set of five questions based on today's lesson and then use them to interview you partner?
52. Can you draw a picture showing what you have learnt today?
53. Can you draw a cartoon strip showing what you have learnt today?
54. Can you draw a cartoon strip showing how you will use today's learning in the future?
55. Can you write a letter to one of next year's students explaining what today's lesson is about?
56. Can you write a speech persuading people that what we have learnt today is important?
57. Can you produce five key points which sum up today's learning?
58. Can you create a mind-map showing what we have learnt today?
59. How might you combine today's learning with something else you already know?
60. What existing skills or knowledge could you combine today's learning with?
61. What criteria would you use to judge whether someone has fully understood the lesson today?
62. How does today's lesson connect to your existing knowledge?
63. How does today's lesson connect to our previous areas of study?
64. How might today's lesson connect to other areas of the curriculum?
65. Swap your work with a partner and assess it: What have they done well? How might they improve?
66. Assess your own work: What have you done well? How might you improve?

67. What strengths have you shown in today's lesson? What areas for improvement can you find?

68. How would you have taught today's lesson and why?

69. What difficulties have you encountered today? How have you dealt with them?

70. What difficulties might a student encounter if they were new to today's topic?

71. Assess your learning using the learning objective: Have you met it? How? If not, what do you still need to do in order to meet it?

72. What evidence do you have showing what you have learnt today?

73. What key question would you ask to find out whether someone has understood today's lesson?

74. How might you translate today's lesson into a graph?

75. How might you explain what we have learnt today using symbols?

76. How might you express what you have learnt today using your body?

77. What do you feel you have gained from today's lesson?

78. What would you like us to study next and why?

79. Why might adults have decided that it is important for young people to know about what we have studied in today's lesson?

80. Where might you use today's learning in the next month?

81. How would you describe your experience of today's lesson using colours and shapes?

82. How useful is what we have learnt today? Why?

83. What is the most important thing we have learnt over the past few lessons and why?

84. Compare what you know now with what you knew at the start of the lesson. How is it different?

85. What different possibilities can you imagine for next lesson, bearing in mind what we have learnt today?

86. Compare what you have learnt this lesson with what you learnt last lesson. How is it similar? How is it different?

87. Can you write a message to an alien explaining what you have learnt today?

88. Can you use symbols to show what you have learnt today?

89. Can you make a model of one aspect of your learning?

90. Can you sculpt one of the key ideas from today's lesson?

Chapter Thirteen – An example of how to create a set of questions around a theme

This chapter provides an example of how to create a set of questions around a specific theme, in this case, the past. As in chapters six through ten, the letter 'X' is used to denote the subject of the question. So, for example:

How might X have been different in the past?

Can become:

How might the reception of Macbeth have been different in the past?

Or:

How might scientific experiments have been different in the past?

Or:

How might graphic design have been different in the past?

And so on.

The question set demonstrates how you can take a theme that is relevant to your subject and look it at from a number of different perspectives. In so doing, you are able to create a collection of questions which can be used again and again, because they are generic.

Here, then, are the questions:

1. How might X have been different in the past?
2. What things may have affected X in the past?
3. How might the passage of time have altered X?
4. Is it possible for us to know what X was like in the past? Why?
5. How might we interpret X, based on what we know about the past?
6. Why might X today be different from X in the past?
7. What is the relationship between X today and X in the past?
8. How might X have changed over time? Why? What might have caused the changes?
9. How might X have stayed the same over time? Why? What might have caused this?
10. How might different elements of X have been affected differently by the passage of time?
11. How might our interactions with X be different today from people in the past?
12. If elements of X were the same in the past as they are today, what are the consequences of this?
13. Can we use our knowledge of X in the past to make predictions about X in the future?
14. How might X have been different if Y had happened?
15. What factors have influenced X's development?
16. Are all cases of X in the past the same? Why? What are the implications of this?
17. How has X been shaped by the past?
18. How has X been shaped by its own past?
19. What similarities can you identify between X today and X in the past?
20. How might X's rate of change have altered over time?

21. Can we use X in the present to work out what X was like in the past? How? How could we test our results?
22. How likely do you think it is that X will stay as it was during the past? What are your reasons for thinking that?
23. What might the history of X tell us about X today?
24. How might X have changed differently over time given different situations or influences?
25. To what extent is X today the same as X in the past? Why? How do you know this? How might you try to test this?

You will notice how 'the past' becomes a focus around which all manner of interesting and engaging questions can be formulated. The technique can be used with any other theme and is not limited to any particular area of the curriculum.

Chapter Fourteen – Conclusion

So there you have it, the complete guide to how to use questioning in the classroom. Of course, no book such as this is ever really complete, and you will add much more to what I have outlined through the course of your own experience.

To draw things to a close, it is worth reminding ourselves of some of the key points teachers should keep in mind when using questioning in the classroom:

- All questions share a set of common traits.
- Questions direct respondents in how to answer.
- Open questions are generally more effective than closed questions.
- The teacher can cultivate the kind of answers they would like through adept use of questioning.
- Thinking carefully and critically about questioning – both written and oral – will help you to teach better. This, in turn, will help your students to make significant progress.

This book offers a wide range of techniques, strategies, activities, ideas and exemplar questions which will help you excel at questioning in the classroom. Use them, reflect on them and adapt them as you see fit. Your teaching will benefit, and so will your students.

There is nothing left to say, other than good luck in your questioning endeavours. Although, perhaps we should end things on a question; what do you think?

Printed in Poland
by Amazon Fulfillment
Poland Sp. z o.o., Wrocław